JOURNEY INTO THE FOG

JOURNEY INTO THE FOG is an account of the life and voyages of Vitus Bering, who in the second quarter of the eighteenth century opened up the North Pacific and established Russia's claim to its fabulous wealth.

It is a story over which hangs fog, of how men live and die and accomplish their purpose while almost blinded by the elements. Everything that was done was determined by luck—usually bad luck. Yet the expedition was a success; it accomplished everything it set out to do. As a result the coasts of Siberia and Alaska were accurately charted for the first time and Russia's claim to this area was firmly established.

Bering worked under odds that seemed almost unsurmountable. Often discredited officially, more often than not without the money to carry on, his spirit alone kept things going until he lost his life on a deserted island off Kamchatka, where the *St. Peter* was shipwrecked. Even his reputation was clouded for years; others received credit for the work he had done; his charts were laughed at because he had sailed across an area which the famous map makers of Europe claimed was not water but land, and though finally a sea was named after him, it has been only in comparatively recent years that the value of his work has been fully recognized.

The voyage of Vitus Bering into the North Pacific was one of the last great voyages of discovery in our physical world; after him there were few unsailed seas. It has all the elements of adventure and of the mysterious oneness of man's battle against the elements. Simply told, this is an unforgettable reading experience.

This story has not been serialized in any form prior to book publication.

JOURNEY INTO THE FOG

THE STORY OF VITUS BERING
AND THE BERING SEA

By Cornelia Goodhue

Half-steam ahead, by guess and lead, for the sun is mostly veiled—
Through fog to fog, by luck and log, sail you as Bering sailed. . . .

RUDYARD KIPLING

GARDEN CITY, N. Y. 1944

DOUBLEDAY, DORAN & COMPANY, INC.

To OTHO

PREFACE

THE ALEUTIANS are a chain of islands stretching from the mainland of America to Siberia. On one side they are exposed to cold winds from the pole, and on the other are washed by the warm Japan current. The temperature difference produces heavy fog through the summer months, and in the winter, when the sea to the north is frozen, an area of permanent cyclone.

Inaccessible in winter and hidden under fog in summer, the islands have little attraction for men, but they offer a haven for sea animals. The seal rookeries of the world are here. It was here that the sea otter lived. The whale and the walrus retreated to the shelter of Bering Sea, and these waters still swarm with salmon and cod. When they were found, these islands meant more to civilized man than the wealth of the Indies.

This story is an account of the expedition which braved the dangers of the fog and discovered what lay in it. It is a story of men who work in fog, who live and die and accomplish their purposes, blind. Nine days out of ten the ships sail in fog, a gray circle of sea which does not change. The great voyage of discovery becomes a passage in time, not space, the great adventure a monotonous waiting. While they wait the commander and half the crews die, exhausted by dangers which have never shown themselves.

Even before the physical fog closed around them, these men were working blind. They fought the wilderness under orders framed in cities. Every plan that was made for them failed. Every turn of this story, everything that is done, is determined by luck—usually bad luck. And yet the expedition was a success; it accomplished everything it set out to do. And that was not luck. Not luck, not forethought, but something without a name today. And that something is more fundamentally us, more vital to our lives, than are our minds.

This is a story of heroism. To accept an impossible order and carry it through to success, to drag the chains and anchors and all the materials for shipbuilding from the Gulf of Finland to the Pacific Ocean, and at the end of such a journey to build ships and sail three thousand miles of unknown water—is this the work of men? But if we come closer and watch the work day by day, there is no glamour. The men who did all this, who endured the hardships of the gods and conquered chaos, are simply working for wages, and pitifully small wages. The great problems of the expedition dissolve into the ever-present problem of food and shelter, of getting along till tomorrow. In a gray frame, on a gray background, we see men like ourselves, breaking under the burdens we break under. And this humdrum, familiar thing is the bricks and mortar of glory. Surely that is a greater thing to know than the fact that our kind has at some time in the past achieved greatness.

Vitus Bering's voyage across the North Pacific in the second quarter of the eighteenth century was the last great voyage of discovery in our physical world. After him there were no unsailed seas. But we who live in the twentieth century are running fast before the wind into another unknown world. This story is offered as an example of how such things are done.

CONTENTS

JOURNEY INTO THE FOG

1. PETER THE GREAT AND THE STRAITS OF ANIAN

IT WAS FOUR O'CLOCK on a January afternoon, 1725. The winter night had already closed in on St. Petersburg. Snowflakes glistened in the lights of sleighs that sped silently through the streets and across the great square to the Winter Palace. A hated czar, who had embroiled his country in unwanted wars, who had broken the power of the princes and undermined the authority of the church, was dying. The lords of Russia were hurrying to his antechamber to prove their loyalty; in the cathedral near by priests were dutifully imploring the Almighty to prolong his life.

No priest had yet been called to the royal bedroom. Here the court physicians had the disagreeable task of asking the czar to prolong his own life. From time to time one would approach the bed and suggest rest or a sedative—only to back away in terror from the curses of the enraged old man. Peter had lived violently—fifty years of war and reform, of violent passions, hard work, and drunkenness—and he did not die quietly. But he had no thought of rebelling against death. In fifty years he had never been swerved from his purpose by begging or flattery, and he supposed that God, his far-off czar, was a being like himself, ruthless in accomplishing his purpose, appreciative of good work, and insulted by wheedling. How else could He have gotten so much done? Peter accordingly put God, and medicine, out of his mind. He called for plans and maps and secretaries.

Peter's life had been spent in wars. He had fought the Turks in the south and the Swedes in the north, to give his country what he called "a window that looks on Europe." He had won outlets on both seas and built a navy. He had built the window. He had made an inland, isolated country one with France and Holland and England. He had also made an Asiatic people European. The Russian of Peter's day prided himself on living as the Holy Apostles had done. The good Russian was contemptuous of worldly things, but he measured the garments in the holy pictures so that his skirt would not be fuller or narrower, longer or shorter, than St. Peter's had been. Because the Byzantine dress was the symbol and the badge of the Byzantine mind, Peter first attacked the dress. He believed that rage was the only answer to stupidity and wasted no time in persuasion. He ordered his people to model their clothes after Louis XV and sent soldiers through the country to enforce this. The soldiers tore the holy garments off women and sent them home naked and beheaded venerable men for having patriarchial beards. When these tactics had brought all but the most powerful princes into line, Peter put a tax on non-conformity and allowed the boyars their beards, at a price.

Peter had done more than break the old mold. He had brought skilled laborers from Europe and taught a few Russians the European arts and crafts. But he had meant to do so much more! All that he had done was merely a clearing of the ground for the things that he had really wanted to do. And there was no one who would willingly carry on this work when he was dead. This was what terrified him, and goaded him, as he lay dying. He must start everything, at once!

In the lighted reception hall of the palace, gentlemen swept plumed hats along a mosaic floor to ladies who curtsied into billowing silk. Around them were high walls hung with tapestries, pastoral scenes in which courtesans played at being shepherdesses. The soft silks and velvets, the pretentious simplicity, the blue forget-me-nots and pink roses of Versailles, set off starkly a few powerful noblemen wearing the straight-cut clothes of old Russia, stiff with pearls and emeralds—proud families that Peter had not been able to subdue. They proved their righteousness, and their power, by their dress.

Feodor Dolgoruk, Bishop of Aransky, an enormous man made even larger by his clerical dress, pushed his way through the crowd. His loud, meaningless laugh echoed over the clatter around him. On the death of the czar the Dolgoruks would be a family to be reckoned with, and Feodor had dreams of becoming Patriarch of Russia. He knew what the difficulties would be. The movement toward new ways and European ideas was strong and some of it would outlive the czar. There were too many young noblemen now who spoke and read French and traveled in Europe, and they were saying that Feodor Dolgoruk was a stupid, overfed boor, and that the Bishop of Novgorod was a cleric who was also educated. Feodor coveted the good will of these advanced young men.

While he was feeling this need acutely, chance put into his hands a German divinity student, a poor scholar looking for patronage in Russia—a colorless, seventeen-year-old boy who said nothing. He was perfectly safe, and his appearance would give the Bishop of Aransky a cosmopolitan air among the people who admired that sort of thing, the people who were saying that the bishop could not read his own bible and who boasted about their visits to Paris. Time was short and Feodor had to make all he could of the boy this evening. He pushed him through the crowd, calling greetings to men he did not know. Where it was least expected he brought his heavy hand down on a shoulder and shouted, "Meet my young friend from Leipzig!"

The boy bowed stiffly to these introductions. "A cat from Leipzig would suit him as well," he told himself. The boy was painfully ill at ease. He was conscious that he was a small man and that he was poorly dressed. Feodor Dolgoruk had recognized this much. But he had not recognized the scorn and hatred in the tightly closed lips. And Feodor had not seen the remarkable intelligence in the boy's restless brown eyes, sharp with interest. Nothing escaped those eyes. The boy saw everything, weighed every detail, without a flicker on his expressionless mouth. "That costume would buy Wittenberg," he told himself. Scanning one lordly face after another, he thought, "Less intelligence than is required of a coachman."

"Alexei Ivanovich, my friend!" The bishop was calling with unusual loudness and waving his arm. A young man turned abruptly toward them, his face shining with laughter.

"Lieutenant Chirikov, the cleverest young man in St. Petersburg!" Feodor boomed, laying his hand on the lieutenant's arm to draw him closer. "I want you to do something for my young friend from Leipzig"—Feodor paused to let the word be heard—"Herr Steller. You must show him, Alexei, that we Russians know how to enjoy ourselves."

The two men bowed. The German understood fully the careless good health in the Russian's face and the fortune in Spanish lace at his wrist. The Russian, to whom Leipzig meant much less than the bishop imagined, wondered what this stiff young man would consider enjoyable. But the thought vanished at once in his natural affability.

At that moment a movement in the crowd brought the two men side by side but took their attention from each other. Around them people were stepping back to clear a passage. Admiral General Count Apraksin was crossing the hall toward the czar's apartments. The courtiers who had made way a few feet ahead of the admiral did not close in behind him as they might have done, but remained motionless, staring after him, so that his passing left a trail of calm like a ship crossing a harbor. A second man was following close behind, and it was this man who held the attention of everyone. He was an unknown European, middle-aged, heavily built. The high boots and striding walk, the straight hair, stiff and burned by the sun, marked him as a soldier and not a diplomat or scholar.

To the courtiers he was a type—the self-confident stranger who had access to the czar's apartments when the lords of Russia had not. The older men stared after him with mixed awe and dislike. The younger men, who had grown up in an atmosphere of respect for Europe, were more curious. They were examining his clothes, his walk, the expression of his face. Racially the stranger was of a type very similar to themselves; their clothes had been made in Europe as his had. What was it then that set him off from them, that made him so obviously a "European" while they so obviously were not?

It was not Europe but the sea that had stamped this man and that set him apart. He knew the vastness and the realities of life, dark waves and changing winds—blind, omnipotent matter and the world of chance where passion and deceit, hopes, fears, threats, and promises meant nothing. The sea was in his rolling walk and in his passive blue eyes that looked out on the world he moved through without an inward glance or shadow of personal bias.

Feodor Dolgoruk smiled hopefully. The czar's friend might know his German protégé, might see him and bow to him! And as he passed, the stranger turned his head. But it was Alexei Chirikov who got the quick glance of recognition. The lieutenant drew himself to attention and bowed. He knew that one of the Danes at Admiral Siever's had recommended him for a position of honor. This must be the one! Chirikov tried vainly to remember what he knew about the man and cursed because these foreign faces were so much alike. George Steller too watched the stranger; he was interested in the type of man who was in demand in Russia. This one wore his clothes well, but they were not well made; he was competent, but probably not educated. "I will be worth more than he is, at his age," he told himself.

The courtiers had held back from the czar's apartments, and for a short space Count Apraksin and his guest walked alone. When they reached the door the admiral hesitated to knock. A sour smile wrinkled his face and he turned to his companion.

"The dangers of the high seas are nothing to the storms you meet in this harbor!" he said warningly.

The door closed behind them. At the far end of the room was the bed, lighted on both sides by torches. The czar sat in the bed against the pillows, turning over papers in his lap. As he lifted his head, Count Apraksin stepped from in front of his companion and announced, "Captain Vitus Bering."

The Dane strode across the room, his eyes fixed on the bed. He saw the feeble hands, the drawn skin, the haggard eyes of the man he had served for twenty years. Peter read the pain in his face and voiced it for him.

"I have very little time!" he said curtly.

For a minute neither spoke. The czar drew a map from among the papers in his lap.

"This was made for me by the house of Delisle, some years ago. And a lot of good it is to anyone!"

The map was largely blank. It showed the coast of Siberia drawn in a straight line north of Korea. East of this lay a large, semicircular country, Japan, and beyond that, open sea. The American coast had not been drawn north of the California peninsula. The blank space of the map pleased Bering; he had expected to find this area filled with imaginary lands.

"They did well to leave this empty," he said. "They know very little about this sea."

"And that little is wrong," said Peter. "My Cossack fur traders have gone far into Siberia—three thousand miles by their own reckoning—and come to an eastern ocean. They have built a port, Okhotsk. East of the Sea of Okhotsk you again find land. This is doubtless a peninsula as Russians have crossed it in the north and again come to the sea. It is called Kamchatka. French geographers tell me this Kamchatka must be part of the western coast of America."

Peter leaned against the pillows and smiled, remembering the time he had spent in Paris with the geographers. "They were an ingenious lot! How they quoted this one and that! And how they wrangled! I discovered that geography was a speculative science, and decided to get my map from Siberia. I intended to present the Academy with a true chart. And we will do that yet!" He sat up again in the bed.

"You are to take thirty men and two officers and cross Siberia. When you reach the sea beyond Kamchatka you will build a boat and follow the coast easterly till you come to a European settlement. Ask the inhabitants the name of the place and put it down in writing. You will then return here and make a chart. Apraksin tells me you have made your arrangements and can start at once."

Cross Siberia and build a boat, follow the coast till you reach a known settlement—simple words spanning incredible labors. Neither man underestimated the difficulties of this work. But it was characteristic of Peter the Great to give amazing orders in amazingly simple words. It was also characteristic of him to select men who could carry out such orders.

Vitus Bering was typical of the men Peter had brought into Russia. The son of a poor family in Jutland, he had gone to sea as a boy. At twenty he entered the Russian navy. A natural intelligence and painstaking, careful work had done the rest. He became a captain and built a home in Finland. Slow-moving and inarticulate, he had the quiet self-confidence of a man used to authority and initiative, coupled with the circumspect deliberateness of a man whose decisions must always be correct. He would never do anything spectacular or admire anything spectacular. Because ambition meant to him the life of the capital, a life of intrigue and favoritism, he supposed that he had no ambition. But now—one quarter of the northern hemisphere, which no competent navigator had ever penetrated—and he was to chart it!

He spoke slowly. "The work which you are giving me is the greatest gift remaining in the world today!"

Peter was embarrassed by thanks. He said sharply, "One of your officers must be a Russian."

Bering's mind was on the magnificence of the venture, on the able men who would be honored to take part in it. He spoke without thinking. "There is no Russian fit for such work."

The czar was angered. "That is why you are taking a Russian. My people must learn. They cannot always depend on *nyemtsui.*" He had used a peasant word for "the foreigner," a word full of hatred and contempt.

It startled Bering out of his reverie. "I have asked for Martin Spanberg——"

Peter nodded. "Spanberg is good."

"—and Alexei Chirikov."

Peter made a grimace. "Chirikov is a good musician!"

Peter did not plan the role George Steller was to play in the voyage to America. In sending out this expedition the czar intended to win certain practical benefits for the Russian Empire, and he selected men who could accomplish this. But he also intended to win the admiration of the learned societies of Europe, and he did not take the necessary steps for that. The scholars would never admire the authors of such work, or the work itself, but only a report from one of their own kind. And Peter did not select a scholar to speak for him. Years later that work would fall to the ambitious George Steller; and it was not the czar, or Vitus Bering, but George Steller, who would receive the admiration of the academies.

Peter took up the papers in his lap. "As you sail east from Kamchatka you may find a strait running north to Hudson's Bay. The English say they can take a ship over America, an easy run from Greenland to the Pacific. The strait is called Anian. I have reports on it here. A Captain Frobisher believed he found such a passage in 1576 but he did not get through. There have been a number of expeditions since, however."

"And none of them got through."

"I don't know that. An English fur company is fighting these investigations and belittling them. But a Greek, Juan de Fuca, took a ship through these straits for Admiral Drake. And more recently an Admiral de Fonte, sailing the west coast of America, found a broad opening at 53. He followed this for twenty days and met a ship from Massachusetts."

"I know about this De Fonte. And I know about Juan de Fuca and Juan de Gama, and the rest of them. They are never able to take their bearings. They never know where they are, and you're left marveling that they found their way home again!"

Bering spoke with the irritation of a man who has been fooled into a great waste of time and labor. He had spent precious hours, snatched between sleep and duty, pondering over these tales. At first exasperated by the vagueness of the reports, he had finally decided that they were unworthy of any navigator—that they were the work of charlatans who preyed on an ignorant public.

Peter allowed him his irritation; he had too often raged over slovenly and inadequate reports himself. But he had other reasons for believing in this strait. "Very well. Very well. But even if these men are all fools—where there are so many stories, there is likely to be something back of them."

"All these tales come from England, and the Englishman's religion is back of them," Bering said. "If God made the world for English merchants He would certainly have made a northwest passage to the East."

Peter laughed. "The English merchants are wonderful. If God didn't make this passage for them they will dig it for themselves. But if He did make it—we will find it and rent it to them! And I think He did make it. I have one report which does not come from England. This is what I principally wanted to tell you. Twice whales have been washed ashore in Kamchatka with harpoons in their bodies. I had the harpoons sent to me. They were made in Holland!"

The hand of western Europe had been laid on eastern Asia. Peter smiled at the amazement and wonder in Bering's eyes. But the talk had exhausted him.

"Here is your authorization," he said abruptly, and sank against the pillows.

Count Apraksin came forward and took the papers which were slipping from the czar's fingers. Bering moved away from the bed. Unwilling to watch the struggle which was taking place there, he stared at the document which had been handed to him. It was an official order from the most powerful sovereign in Europe, putting the whole strength of the

Russian Empire at his disposal, and it was also a plain message from a great man.

To THE GOVERNORS OF SIBERIA:

We are sending Captain Vitus Bering to Siberia to undertake a naval expedition. If he comes to you and asks help of one kind or another, you are to give it to him.

PETER

Peter remembered that he was dying. His wife Catherine would succeed him to the throne, and she would attempt to carry out his policies. But she would be weak, and after her— all things were possible. Peter had boasted that Russia would outshine France in her contributions to science, and perhaps this, his only contribution, was being started too late. It might be thwarted by his successors. He spoke wistfully.

"I will not live to hear what you discover, or to see you through this. But if you do send a chart to the French Academy—we will both have done something for science."

"The chart will be sent." Bering wanted to swear the most sacred oath that ever crossed a man's lips. Struggling for the words, which he could not find, he said, "So long as I live— your will lives in me!"

Peter smiled. "God bless you, Vitus—Petrovitch."

2. EASTERN SIBERIA

THE PORT of Okhotsk, which Peter had spoken of so confidently, proved to be the cabins of eleven fishermen. But by the time Bering reached it he had come to expect such populations. Twelve hundred miles from St. Petersburg, and just east of the Urals, was Tobolsk, the capital of Siberia and a true metropolis. Two thousand miles from Tobolsk was Yakutsk, the capital of Eastern Siberia and a town of five hundred. Between lay forests, steppes, and tundra, and at long intervals "cities" of thirty or forty inhabitants, the headquarters of traders and trappers.

Eastern Siberia was a territory of unknown boundaries and unknown peoples. According to a Yakutsk census report, there were in the province ten thousand natives who paid tribute to the Russian government, one thousand government officials who collected this tribute, and one hundred settlers—criminal and political exiles. There were also wandering bands of robbers who were not listed by the census. Robbers and tax collectors were intermingling groups. Both were fur traders. But the robber preyed on Russians as well as natives and kept everything he got, while the tax collector surrendered part of his booty to the man above him and in return received guns and ammunition from the government supplies.

Bering reached Yakutsk in the summer of 1726 and remained there only a few weeks. Seven hundred miles of mountain passes lay between Yakutsk and the sea, but the expedition reached Okhotsk that winter. The following spring they built a ship to ferry them to Kamchatka.

These men from the docks at St. Petersburg had trudged over steppes and tundra and cut their way through forests, pulling heavy wagons through mud and snow and along swift mountain streams. They had dragged the chains and anchors and cannon and all the materials for shipbuilding from the Gulf of Finland to the Pacific Ocean. After two years of inhuman labor they again had blue water, wet winds, and the smell of the sea.

By the second week in July they were ready to embark. The earth huts which they had built to shelter them through the previous winter were crumbling in the spring rains. A ship

stood in the bay, her sails set. The makeshift village was filled
with the confusion of leaving. Men were wandering in groups
along the beach or searching the abandoned barracks for personal belongings.

Chirikov had been looking for Bering or Spanberg, and he
found them together on the ship. They were bending over a
map, discussing the voyage. The Danes never consulted him.
They seemed to forget that he too was an officer. Chirikov
was hurt but not resentful. He felt embarrassingly young in
their company, and apologetic for interrupting them.

"There's a monk, Kossirefski, who wants to go to Kamchatka. To visit some converted natives, he says. He claims to
know all about the waters around here."

Bering and Spanberg looked up with interest.

"But I should warn you—I don't trust him. He knows all
the worst scoundrels on the expedition."

"That is the business of a priest," said Bering.

Chirikov laughed. "That is just what he said! Shall I bring
him in?"

The monk was unduly ingratiating; he fawned and flat-
tered and had the peasant's trick of evading a question by not
understanding it and answering with a flow of irrelevancies
and apologies for his stupidity. But he was very anxious to get
to Kamchatka and willing to pay for this with solid information. When the questions were not about himself, but about
the country they were going through, his manner changed;
he spoke clearly, to the point, and with great assurance. Bering watched this shift of character and knew that the man
himself was unaware of it.

"Kossirefski? You are from Poland?" he asked.

"No sir. No. I am a native of Siberia. Alas, I am not so for-
tunate! God has given me a barren life, in keeping with my
powers. . . ."

But Bering decided that the obvious deceit in this man was

a cover for his intelligence—for some reason he found it convenient to be considered stupid. No man had to hide his crimes in Siberia.

"I would like to see you handle the ship," he said.

The *Fortune* was anchored beyond the sandspit, and beyond was open sea without headlands of any kind. Kossirefski took charge while Bering and Spanberg watched. He was still intent on his work several hours after the flat dunes of Okhotsk had sunk into the horizon. Several times Bering saw shallow water after they had cleared it.

"You know a great deal about a ship," he said.

The monk shrugged his shoulders. "I know a great deal about these waters. I know every foot of the bottom here. I wish you'd let me take you round Kamchatka, since we both want to get to the eastern coast."

"I do not know certainly that this is a peninsula——"

"I do. I've rounded it several times."

The wind was in the sails. Bering looked across the flat expanse of sea longingly. This was his natural element; this was the way to transport men and supplies, not against the obstacles of the land—rivers, mountains, swamps, and ice.

"The overland journey will be six hundred miles," Kossirefski urged.

Bering shook his head. The risk was too great. "The *Fortune* was not built for the open sea," he said.

While at sea Kossirefski made a map of Kamchatka for them. Bering and Spanberg watched him work. His sureness, his careful detail, amazed them. "You're a first-class navigator!" Spanberg cried enthusiastically. "What are you doing in this beggar's costume?" But with that question the competent Kossirefski disappeared and left only the voluble, cringing, unmanageable peasant.

He had told them what to expect on Kamchatka. There were about a hundred Russians in the country, recently banded together under a leader who called himself governor although there was no government in Kamchatka and no tribute reached St. Petersburg. These men wintered in two settlements, called simply the Upper and the Lower Posts. There was another, nameless settlement on the west coast at the mouth of the Bolshaya River, and it was here that the ship would anchor. To cross Kamchatka one followed the rivers. Three hundred miles up the Bolshaya, a short portage brought one to the Upper Post at the headwaters of the Kamchatka River. The journey down the Kamchatka to the Lower Post, at its mouth, was also three hundred miles. The governor was at the Upper Post.

The *Fortune* anchored at the mouth of the Bolshaya. This settlement was fourteen huts. Winter came almost immediately, hiding rivers, trails, and brush with a cover of snow. To remain where they were meant several months' hard labor building shelters. Bering decided to use that labor pushing on to the Upper Post. He thought he knew what he would find there—Russians less civilized than the natives and, like them, living in mud huts and eating raw fish. But it was a large settlement; there would be shelter of some kind and additional hands to help him get his supplies along the route. He thought that by assuming the governor was really a governor and the fur traders under him really tax collectors he could frighten them into doing what he asked. Putting Spanberg in charge of the train which was slowly moving up the river and taking Chirikov with him, Bering went ahead by dog team to prepare the way. Kossirefski, who had remained at camp in the hope of just this, went with them as guide.

On the sixth day of travel Kossirefski stopped the team and climbed out of the sled. "You leave the river here," he explained. "I am going further east, but you will find your way without any trouble."

When Bering and Chirikov had climbed the bank they

looked back at Kossirefski. He stood on the ice of the river, his shoulders huddled inside his heavy coat, his skirts flapping in the wind. Chirikov had seen nothing in this man beyond the fact that he was a charlatan, and had stopped thinking about him. If he thought about him at all at this moment, he supposed that he knew where he was going and how to get there. But Bering, seeing that lonely black figure against the white wilderness, suddenly felt a great pity for the man. Where he was going, or what he was going from, Bering did not know. But he was flesh and blood, frail stuff to fight the elements alone.

"Are you sure you want to go alone?" he asked. "Hadn't you better come to the post with us?"

The monk smiled—a frank, open smile, completely at his ease for the first time. "I like it better here."

Two hours after leaving the river, Bering and Chirikov reached the Upper Post. It was a stockaded village, visible for miles across the flat expanse of snow. As they drew near, Bering saw the huge trees of the paling and said, "There is timber for shipbuilding here."

Chirikov felt an abyss open at his feet. Had they come four thousand miles, through two years of horrible labor, without knowing whether it would be possible to build a ship or not?

"Don't you think about those things ahead of time?" he asked.

"I don't think till I've something to think on," Bering answered.

Chirikov was not wholly satisfied. "What do you do then—when you aren't doing anything else?"

Bering understood the question. "I look at the world." He waved his arm at the whiteness around them.

A sentry took their papers before allowing them to drive in. Inside the stockade were Russian log cabins. Dogs penned in various parts of the village yelped savagely at the strange team. Russian men in fur coats and hoods stood before the cabins, staring at them, but no one spoke. There was no greeting of any kind beyond the barking of the dogs. The sentry led them to a large building in the center of the village and told them to wait there for the governor.

The room which they had entered had no windows and was lighted only by a fire on the hearth. Blinded by the snow, they were unable for some time to make out their surroundings, but as the room grew clearer they stared about them in amazement. This room would have seemed crude enough in St. Petersburg. It was unplastered, without windows, without ornaments, and the only furniture was a table and three chairs. But since leaving Tobolsk, more than two years before, these men had seen no plaster. Mud floors, bark-covered walls, guns, traps, and skins had come to be the expected thing. Here on the outskirts of the world, in Kamchatka itself, they had expected even less. The room they were in was floored with wood, and on the floor lay a heavy Chinese carpet. The walls had been planed smooth and stained. The seats and backs of the three chairs were upholstered, and on the table in the center of the room were books and a lute.

Both men were disturbed by the luxury about them. Bering had supposed that he knew the sort of man he had to deal with. He had not expected this and no longer knew what to expect. The room brought back to Chirikov the life he had stepped out of two years before—two terrible long years in which he had forgotten that life could be anything but hunger and cold and fatigue. Now the soft pressure of the rug under his heavy boots reminded him of perfumes and rustling silks. He took the lute from the table and ran his fingers across the strings. The soft world of gaiety and romance was still alive and breathing under his hands!

Lost to everything about him, Chirikov sat on the floor and took the instrument between his knees. His hands, cracked and hardened by the hemp ropes of harnesses and the iron cables of the barges, would not bend to the chords; his rough fingers fumbled on the strings. He rocked his body in exasperation; then he gave up the chords and plucked a melody. Soon he began to sing—a song as sweet and delicate as the tones of the lute:

> *I know many bits of wisdom,*
> *This I know with perfect sureness:*
> *Lives of seal are free and merry,*
> *Feeding on incautious salmon.*

Bering watched his lieutenant curiously. In the two years spent battling their way across Siberia he had hardly given him a thought. Now he was suddenly aware of the matted hair, the bronzed face covered with a heavy beard, the mud-caked clothes of Cossack traders, and the bright, burning eyes of half-starved men. Looking at this and hearing the incongruous, beautiful little song, his heart ached for the carefree boy he had plunged so deeply into hardship.

> *If this knowledge is too little,*
> *I can tell you other matters:*
> *Whitings live in quiet shallows,*
> *Salmon love the level bottom.*

Chirikov put down the lute and groaned.

"Go on. Go on. That is well done." The words were spoken in French, in a rich, soft voice. The two men turned and faced their host.

A chair mounted on wheels had been pushed into the room. In it sat an old man wrapped in blankets. For a moment Bering saw only the scar which puckered the face before him —the brand of the exile to Siberia.

Chirikov had risen to his feet. Staring at the man before him, he whispered, "General Pissarjev!"

Bering knew the name—a Russian nobleman who had at one time been president of the War College. And he understood the man—an arrogance which neither political disgrace nor the poverty of Siberia could touch. Stripped of everything that had supported him, old, crippled, and an outcast, by the sheer violence of his will, he still made himself feared and obeyed.

Pissarjev waved his hand toward the chairs. "Excuse me for not rising; the St. Petersburg jailers have made that difficult." He spoke with a suave courtliness, meant to intimidate his guests. "I understand you came here with Ivan the Pole." As neither man answered or seemed to understand him, he added, "You left him at the river?"

"Brother Kossirefski?" asked Chirikov.

"A beast, under any name. If there is foul work anyplace in Siberia, he appears. Like a buzzard over carrion. I wonder what brings him to Kamchatka."

Pissarjev went on talking. He told all the evil that he knew of Kossirefski, speaking with an amused, trivial flow of words, as if his only purpose was to be entertaining. "And how he gets about! Once he went south among the islands and set up a kingdom of his own, only to find that he was in the Japanese Empire and had better come back! And you know, he *recommends* killing tax collectors. I'm not a timid man myself, but I wouldn't go that far—that is, I wouldn't recommend it."

Chirikov leaned forward, his arms on his knees, fascinated by the general's story, thoroughly enjoying the juxtaposition of a St. Petersburg scandalmongering manner and hard, Siberian facts. Bering was uncomfortable. One did not cross Kamchatka for this kind of talk.

When Pissarjev paused to laugh at his story, Bering said bluntly, "You have seen our papers. You know our mission. I have come ahead of my men to make arrangements for wintering here."

"Perhaps I am slow-witted, but I do *not* understand your mission. Are you on a naval expedition in Siberia?"

Bering understood the mockery but did not know how to deal with it. He looked at Chirikov. As the younger man said nothing, Bering went on in his own manner.

"We are here under orders from St. Petersburg. As you can see, the governors of Siberia are required to give me whatever assistance I need. And I need to bring my men to this settlement for the winter."

"And as you can see, I am not a Siberian governor! And I owe nothing to St. Petersburg!" Pissarjev had dropped the pretense of politeness, and his voice rang. "I understand your naval expedition. You will build ships on the eastern coast of Kamchatka and go looking for Japan. When you find it the Japanese fur traders will follow you back and ruin the country for us. I see no reason for helping you in any way!"

Chirikov, realizing that the talk which had been polite was now threatening, suddenly responded to the look which Bering had given him. He said gently, "We are not going to Japan, sir. Our mission is to satisfy certain personal interests of the czar."

"That is very curious." Pissarjev resumed his courtly manner. "You know the czar hates the sea, and everything that smells of it! He refuses to remain in St. Petersburg because it stinks of salt water and ships."

Without stopping to wonder if the old man were demented, Chirikov asked angrily, "Have you been in touch with His Majesty recently? He is dead, you know."

"So he is. And the Swedish trollop who succeeded him is dead too. Did you know that? The little Alexevitch is czar. They tell me he is devoted to Ivan Dolgoruk. I hope to be in touch with him very soon."

For a moment no one spoke. Far away in St. Petersburg their expedition had probably been forgotten. But if it was remembered, orders might be sent out for them to return. Here at the edge of the world, with the hardships of the journey behind them, they might have to turn back with nothing accomplished. Such a messenger might be on his way even now, might be waiting at Yakutsk for the spring thaw!

Bering stood up quickly. They must reach the sea, even through these Arctic snows, build their boat, and be gone before a messenger could overtake them.

"We will not make any camp this winter," he said. "If we keep going we can reach the sea by spring. Otherwise it would be another summer before the ship is launched." He turned to Chirikov. "We will start back to the men at once."

Pissarjev smiled. "I believe there is a recent order forbidding cutting timber for the navy, but perhaps it does not apply in Siberia."

Chirikov turned angrily on the old man in the chair. "There are strong men in St. Petersburg who know the Dolgoruks. They will save Russia in spite of a silly child!"

"God in His wisdom has put Russia in the hands of a silly child," Pissarjev said warningly. "And you will meet these strong men in Siberia as you return."

3. THE VOYAGE OF THE
"ST. GABRIEL"

THE *ST. GABRIEL* sailed from the mouth of the Kamchatka in July 1728 and, keeping a few miles from shore, followed the coast, which bore north. It was a rocky, treeless coast; snow-capped mountains rose directly from the water, their sides as straight as a wall. The sea was full of whales and walruses.

Each day brought fog. Sometimes it lay heavy on the ship, a gray-green smother, and the men working in the dripping riggings saw one another as shadowy masses. When the thickness hid the shore four or five miles away it was called "fog" and the *St. Gabriel* moved out to sea. When it thinned it was called "cloudy" and the men resumed their work. They sounded constantly, and the officers were on deck at all hours, taking the bearings of every cove and mountain peak.

For two weeks the coast bore north; the expected turn to the east did not appear. But they were sailing through small, shallow waves which resembled a sea rather than an ocean, and the bottom grew steadily shallower, so the hope of finding land north and east of them remained. On August eleventh they saw land stretching across the northern horizon and followed it east. On the sixteenth this land bore south and the *St. Gabriel* was at last pointed for the Spanish possessions in America. But on the twenty-first they had open sea to the east; the coast turned abruptly north and west.

That day they saw eight Chukchi in a leather boat. One of the Chukchi, using seal bladders to buoy him, swam to the ship. This man was familiar with Russian traders and talked to them through the Koriak whom they had taken as interpreter. He told them that the coast continued north only a short distance and then turned west. He also told them of a large island lying directly ahead in the east. The *St. Gabriel* moved on. They sighted the island, St. Lawrence, and continued north.

They were now approaching the known latitude of the Kolyma River, where it empties into the Arctic Ocean, and when, on August twenty-fourth, they saw the coast turn sharply west, as the Chukchi had told them, the hope of reaching America by this route was lost.

Chirikov and Spanberg were in the bow, taking observations of the promontory, when Bering joined them. He had brought his papers with him.

"We are at 65°30'," he said. "I believe we have reached the most easterly point of Siberia. And that is borne out by the statements of the Chukchi. But the waves here, and the shallow bottom, suggest land in the east. If this land joins Siberia, we might sight it by sailing north. The question is, how much further can we go without risking the ship? Or should we return to Kamchatka now?"

Spanberg had his answer ready. "I think we could safely take three days. If we turn back on the twenty-seventh we will reach Kamchatka before winter. And we have come so close to the Arctic, I think we should try to reach it. I think we should go on to 66°30', if we can do that in three days."

Bering looked at Chirikov. The lieutenant motioned toward the land. "I think our instructions require that we follow this coast without questioning. If it continues west we will come to the mouth of the Kolyma, and that will show that Asia and America are not joined. If the coast turns north—I think we should follow it for about two weeks, and then prepare to winter wherever we find ourselves at that time. We have provisions for a year, and I certainly don't think we should return to Kamchatka without having accomplished anything."

Bering and Spanberg were looking at him in amazement.

"Have you noticed that there are no trees on this coast? Are we to winter in rock and snow?" Spanberg asked.

"There might be forests further on. And we *could* winter in the ship."

"And when the ship breaks up we *could* go home on the ice floes!" Spanberg was angry.

Bering spoke more kindly. "It's out of the question, Alexei

Ivanovich. I couldn't expose the ship to such a risk. Perhaps we would have to touch at the Kolyma to prove that Asia and America are not united. But that is pretty obvious already. As for our instructions—we are looking for American settlements. You don't suggest we sail west over Siberia for that, do you?"

The day was calm and cloudy and the *St. Gabriel* lay at 65°30′ north latitude. Less than thirty miles away, in the fog, stood the headlands of America. But even Chirikov did not suggest that they turn the *St. Gabriel* east to the open sea. Such a voyage required different orders and a different ship. They left the land and sailed north for two days. On August twenty-sixth they had reached 67°18′ without sighting anything.

"You see now that Asia and America are not joined, don't you?" Bering asked Chirikov.

On all sides was gray water and a gray sky. The lieutenant laughed good-humoredly. "No. I don't see anything at all."

They turned back and on August twenty-eighth were again in the strait between America and Siberia. The day was cloudy and there was a good breeze. They sighted Diomede Island and saw a boat of natives, who apparently were not Chukchi and fled at sight of the ship. They continued south.

Fifty years later an Englishman, James Cook, sailed into these waters, following Bering's tracks. He carried Bering's logs and reports in his deckhouse. He compared his own observations with Bering's and was constantly amazed by the accuracy of his predecessor's work. He too was charting the Siberian coast and saw only what Bering had seen. But at 65° 57′ a pale sunlight fell on the deck. A few minutes later the American headlands loomed through the thinning mist. The fog cleared, and under a sunny sky Cook saw the white-topped cliffs of Asia and America facing across a stretch of blue water. He looked at Bering's log. He saw the cloudy skies of August twenty-fourth and twenty-eighth and he saw the freshening breeze which had left the channel clear on the twenty-ninth.

"That was bad luck!" said James Cook, who knew more about luck than most men.

The *St. Gabriel* moved south, checking the observations of a month before. Again they met natives, four boatloads of Chukchi, who came to the ship with meat, fresh fish, fresh water, foxskins, and walrus tusks to sell. The Chukchi were questioned by the Koriak interpreter and said that they traveled from this coast to the mouth of the Kolyma by deer and not by boat.

The officers looked at one another in surprise. The inference was that there was no sea route to the Kolyma. But Bering was not satisfied.

"They have only said that this is their practice. They have not said it is impossible to go by boat. Ask them why they make the journey by deer."

But it now appeared that the interpreter did not speak the Chukchi language! So far he had gotten his information by some other device, and this question was too difficult for him. He could only repeat that the Chukchi traveled by deer.

On September eleventh the *St. Gabriel* ran into a storm which almost proved too strong for her. The main and foresail split and tangled in the rigging; the anchor cable broke and the anchor was lost. But the storm passed, and two days later she reached port at the mouth of the Kamchatka.

The winter was spent on Kamchatka repairing the *St. Gabriel* and trapping for fresh food. Evidences of America came to them everywhere. They found along the shore trunks of large fir trees which did not grow in Kamchatka. Birds of passage came from the east. The natives told them that on a clear day land could be seen in the east.

Bering worked over his report, checking his figures and re-

drawing his charts. He had established the boundaries of Siberia. But other work remained to be done, the uncharted
seas called him, and he ended his report with a recommenda-
tion.

"It is my opinion that America, or some land this side of it,
is not very far from Kamchatka, perhaps a hundred and fifty
or two hundred miles. If that is so, commercial relations with
that country that would be to the advantage of the Russian
Empire could be established. This matter can be investigated
if a vessel is built of from forty-five to fifty tons' burden. It
would also be desirable to map the northern coast of Siberia
and find a sea route to Japan from Kamchatka.

"If the Admiralty is interested in this matter, ships should
be built in Kamchatka and not at Okhotsk, because the necessary timber is here, fish and game are plentiful, and the natives
are well disposed. The mouth of the Kamchatka is deeper and
offers better shelter . . ."

But plans were not in place, and Bering knew that they
were not. Pissarjev had told him that the Dolgoruks were in
power and the Admiralty weak. He would have to show a
conservative Senate solid profit from the first expedition if he
was to get backing for a second.

Accordingly, the following June he left the coast and sailed
east for three days, hoping to sight the land the Kamchatkans
said was there. They had fog continually and sailed in a small
sea. On the second day they passed close to a rocky island
without sighting it. And that was bad luck indeed! This island
was to be the grave of Vitus Bering, and the only American
soil he ever set foot on.

Having seen nothing but mist and water, they returned to
Kamchatka and followed the coast back to Okhotsk, making
a map of the peninsula. Bering felt that this, together with his
map of the northern shores, gave him a great deal to show the
Senate. The journey back across Siberia, unhampered by sup-

plies, was accomplished in six months and they reached Tobolsk the following January. From here on there were roads,
taverns, and news.

Bering had been away five years, and he asked anxiously
about affairs in St. Petersburg. What he learned confirmed the
worst that Pissarjev had hoped. The Dolgoruks held everything; the Admiralty was only a name. The men he asked
about had died or been sent to exile.

"Count Apraksin is dead, and the czar will not appoint
another president of the Admiralty."

"Peter's navy has rotted in the docks."

While he asked, south of them at the Dolgoruks' palace in
the Ukraine the twelve-year-old czar lay dying of smallpox.
But no news of this probable shift of power had reached
Tobolsk.

THE GREAT KAMCHATKA EXPEDITION

---

4. THE ACADEMY OF SCIENCE
AND THE UNKNOWN WORLD

THE RETURNING EXPEDITION reached St. Petersburg in March 1730, when the young czar had been dead four weeks. A cousin, Anna Ivanovna, was to succeed him, and preparations were being made for her coronation in Moscow. Bering made his report to a bewildered and terrified Senate.

Anna Ivanovna was a middle-aged woman who had lived in poverty all her life, writing begging letters to her relatives. She had been given the throne because the Senate believed she was weak and would be easy to control. But Anna controlled the Senate more thoroughly than Peter had ever done. Poverty and humiliation had not weakened her, but toughened her. She had no shame; there was nothing she would not stoop to to accomplish her ends. And the only end she knew was personal aggrandizement. She made one of the most unscrupulous and one of the pettiest rulers in the history of Europe.

Anna admired Europe, but not the Europe that Peter had

admired. Where Peter had built ships and canals, Anna heated her palace so that orange trees would bloom through a St. Petersburg winter. Where Peter had brought to Russia craftsmen, navigators, and engineers, Anna gathered round her daring theoreticians. Peter had wanted to change Russia; Anna wanted to disown it. She brought with her a European lover and a court of European adventurers. She made princes of the great houses of Russia court buffoons to entertain her European friends. She made an Apraksin caretaker of a rabbit, and married a Golitsuin to a circus monster

The Senate considered Bering's report for two years without reaching a conclusion. The late Admiral Apraksin's memoranda showed that Bering had been ordered to sail until he reached a European settlement. As he had not done this, the Senate felt that he had not carried out his orders and refused to pay his salary.

The newly created Academy of Science, young students from the German universities, also studied the report and found that it showed "a singular disregard of literary niceties." The Academy did not feel that Bering should have followed the coast to California, since the coast did not lead to California, but they did feel that he should have followed it west to the Kolyma River. Not having done this, he had not proven that Asia and America were separate continents, and so had accomplished nothing.

Bering understood the Senate. They considered his expedition worthless because it had added no territory to the Russian Empire. He did not understand the Academy at all. Like Peter, he was interested in trade routes and national boundaries. The Academy, on the other hand, had found a nice problem in geography which was of interest to map makers but not to any user of maps at that time. If Peter, from the skies, heard these arguments, if he heard men wrangling over the earth under the polar ice while California and Japan were still to be found,

his laughter surely shook heaven. But Bering, walking in the
streets of St. Petersburg, could not laugh. As long as the
argument lasted his salary remained unpaid, and he was not a
rich man. And he had to answer these charges which he could
not understand.

The arguments of the Academy harassed Bering as long as
he lived and clouded his name for two centuries after. The
charge that he had been remiss in not following the coast west
to the Kolyma was repeated for seventy years. By 1800 it was
obvious that if the *St. Gabriel* had attempted this she would
have been crushed in the ice. But by 1800 it was also obvious
that if Bering had exposed the ship to an even greater risk by
sailing east he would have found America in a few hours—and
he was thereafter blamed for not having done that.

Bering had taken a brig into the Arctic and had brought it
back—evidence of a man who habitually did the right thing.
Had he done any of a number of things which he did not do,
the adventure would have ended in the silence which closes
most of the early expeditions to the Arctic. But the mistakes
which Bering had not made were not listed in his report, and
the Academy knew nothing of that world of infinite choice
where mistakes are final. They lived in a tidy, reasonable world
of their own invention, and the only mistakes they knew could
be erased.

With the easy self-confidence of men who do not pay for
their errors, they set about to remedy the defects of the first
Kamchatka expedition. The Senate was interested in the North
Pacific, but the Academy of Science was interested in everything, and between them they drew plans for a second expedition which was to embrace everything. And although they
saw nothing good in the work which Bering had already done,
they put him in charge of the greater expedition they were
planning.

While the Senate was busy drawing plans for the Great Kamchatka Expedition, Bering was sent to Moscow to learn from Professor Delisle about the sea routes between Asia and America. He found a note from Professor Delisle waiting for him on his arrival and was astonished by its courteous tone, so in contrast to the imperiousness of the Senate. Joseph Delisle was honored by this opportunity to discuss the North Pacific with Captain Bering; he was afraid the profit from the meeting would be all his; he hoped Lieutenant Chirikov would accompany Captain Bering, and he would arrange to have Father Ignatius present.

Chirikov arrived at Bering's rooms in the early evening. He was wearing a cape of heavy broadcloth and carried a feathered hat and gold-topped cane. He had spent the afternoon at a reception given in honor of one of the German scholars, and pleasure and amusement were still in his face. Bering had not seen him since they reached St. Petersburg the year before and could hardly believe this elegant gentleman was his old lieutenant. He put his hands on Chirikov's shoulders.

"My son! Equally at home in a Yakut hut or a fashionable drawing room. That is greatness!"

Chirikov laid his hat and cane on the table and laughed. "I am not at home in Moscow. And the Yakuts are not as strange as these men from the universities. Have you met them yet?"

He sat down and laughed again at some memory of the afternoon. "The worst of the lot is certainly this George Steller—a beardless baby who can tell you what God did before he made the world. But you will see for yourself. He wants to go with us to Kamchatka."

"To Kamchatka? What can he do?"

"I shall ask him sometime what he can't do. He's a priest, and a physician, and a naturalist—anything you want except good company. But I do hope he goes. He would learn so much from scurvy!"

"What do these gentlemen say about our expedition?" Bering asked bluntly.

Chirikov moved uncomfortably. "I should warn you— there's a great deal these men don't know. They know how the world moves through the stars, but they don't know how a wagon moves through mud. Or a ship through ice. They know the name of every leaf that grows. But they don't know Gregory Pissarjev."

He sat up suddenly with a new light in his face. "I have news for you! I have it from a reliable source that Pissarjev will be made governor of Kamchatka. The Senate believes he may be pardoned and wants to be on both sides of every shift. So they are telling one another that he is such a resourceful man, and so familiar with Eastern Siberia!" Chirikov laughed heartily. "When we get there again we will have him in charge!"

Bering was neither surprised nor amused. The Senate had sent him, the only man who knew the North Pacific, to learn about those waters from Joseph Delisle; it was not surprising that they should make Gregory Pissarjev a governor; nothing that the Senate did could surprise him.

"We can think about that when we are closer to it," he said wearily. "But you were talking about the Academists. I would like to know what they are saying before I meet Professor Delisle this evening."

"It is mostly unpleasant," Chirikov warned. "For example, they say it was not worth while sending us to Kamchatka to bring back the opinions of the Chukchi."

"The Chukchi live there! Should we have brought back the opinions of the English?"

Chirikov shrugged his shoulders. "This George Steller says that we never lost sight of the shore except in a fog!"

"We were charting the shore! Our instructions were to follow the shore. And the *St. Gabriel* couldn't put to sea."

"I know. But he doesn't! He says that to an eager, waiting world we brought back only a chart."

"Only a chart!" Bering's blue eyes shone in amazement. "Only a chart? What more could we bring? We went for a chart." He began to pace the room. "A chart is just what De Gama and De Fuca and the rest of them did not bring. What do these scholars want? More stories of men who stew their meat in gold pots?"

Chirikov knew no more than Bering what the Academy expected. But he had one more thing to say, the force of which he did know.

"They say your chart was not well made."

"My chart was correctly made!"

"I suppose we will learn about that at Professor Delisle's this evening."

Bering was worried. "I have a note from Professor Delisle. It is very courteous and cordial. He wants us to meet a Father Ignatius. Do you know him?"

Chirikov looked up with interest at the mention of this celebrity. "I would like to know him. He's a missionary priest from Siberia. He works with the natives and takes care of the aged and sick. He's in Moscow marketing furs to finance the work."

"Why should we be interested in him?"

"Everybody's interested in him! He's been everywhere and seen the most interesting things."

Joseph Delisle was a timid and sincerely humble man. For forty years he had lived in awe of his astute and scholarly brother William. Now that William was dead the responsibilities of the greatest name among the map makers of Europe were his. He faced his duties bravely, but without confidence.

He was agitated over this meeting with the officers from the North Pacific. There would be valuable information here which he must get for the house of Delisle before it was picked up by some German scholar. But obtaining true information from sea captains was not an easy matter. Their reports had to be carefully weighed and trimmed.

Joseph received his guests in his study. It was a large, richly furnished room; gilt and brocaded satin and white marble glittered in the light of a hundred candles. He greeted them effusively and tried to direct his remarks to Bering. But the captain's impassive face disturbed him and he was forced to turn to Chirikov, who smiled and nodded whenever he was spoken to.

Joseph introduced his brother Louis, a languid young man wearing the most elaborate Parisian clothes.

"My brother has been in Baffin's Bay," Joseph said proudly.

"Why were you in Baffin's Bay?" asked Chirikov.

"Why?" Louis stared at them with protruding eyes. "Why not? I had to be somewhere!"

The stupid answer pleased Chirikov. Why hadn't he answered the Academists in that way? He was at once drawn to this very fashionable man, who like himself had lived in the wilderness and been spoiled for fashion. He followed him across the room.

"You were in Kamchatka," Louis said abruptly. "Why?"

"I was looking for Baffin's Bay."

Joseph was alarmed to see them move away. Seating himself near Bering, he began to explain his brother. "He is a true genius! Don't you agree with me, that one may recognize the type even before it has done the work that will justify it in the eyes of the world? Those erratic, high-strung individuals, who are carried onward by the zeal for life, who never do the practical thing, who go to the farthest corners of the earth but turn back just a few miles before they would have found what all the world wants to know, who see and know all the strange wonders but can't be made to keep a notebook or take their observations accurately. We, the plodders, have to pick up what they drop and piece it together as we can."

Bering's face darkened at this picture of genius. Joseph Delisle said hastily, "By plodders I meant we cartographers. I feel that the work of a navigator is as vital as it is difficult."

A servant announced Father Ignatius, and the four men got to their feet. Joseph Delisle was relieved. He felt that from now on the talk would be easier. But when the priest stood in the doorway an unnatural stillness came over the room and Joseph knew that something was wrong. The hush was broken by a loud laugh from Chirikov.

"Brother Kossirefski!" There was an insulting familiarity in his tone.

"You know the fellow?" asked Louis. The saint and navigator had bored him, but a fake roused his interest.

"Under any name!" said Chirikov. "And I'll guarantee he didn't wear the tonsure when he went to Siberia. Did you?"

"No," said the priest humbly, "I didn't. I was born there."

Joseph Delisle was alarmed. He felt there was a misunderstanding. "In the Eastern Church it is usual to take a religious name——" he began.

Bering was also alarmed. Saint or scoundrel, at the moment Kossirefski was a fashionable holy man. It would be extremely dangerous to try to unmask him. "You may form what opinions you please in Siberia, but do not defend them in Moscow," he said sternly to his lieutenant.

Desperately seizing on the only topic he felt would hold their attention, Joseph Delisle began to talk about geography. "Perhaps you gentlemen would like to see the map I am making of the North Pacific. The Senate has asked me to prepare a map showing the shortest route between Asia and America. To answer them quickly, I could say the farther north one goes, the shorter the route!" Joseph smiled, pleased with his joke.

He led them to the far end of the room, talking rapidly all the while. "I believe one might reach America by sailing east from Kamchatka, as Captain Bering's evidence suggests. But whether one would meet with new lands or new seas on this route is not easy to say, because no one has ever been there. One is equally in the dark as to how far in a northwesterly direction America extends. I feel one could find more quickly the lands seen by De Gama south of Kamchatka, and if anyone should wish to attempt a journey to America by way of these shores, I could furnish all the necessary information so that no mistake might be made."

He had led them to a large map pinned on a drawing table. Bering bent over the map with interest. It differed greatly from the one William Delisle had made for Peter fifteen years before. The distance between Japan and America was now filled with a country called Gamaland. The Kamchatka peninsula had been drawn on the Siberian coast, but it stretched far to the south and was called Yesso.

Joseph was explaining the map. "You will see that I have shown Japan as an island. Japanese sailors, wrecked on Kamchatka and brought to Moscow for questioning a few years ago, said that one traveled from Japan to China by land. But the Jesuit Fathers who have been there insist that it is an island."

He moved his hand further along the paper. "The shores seen by Juan de Gama, which I have located opposite Kamchatka, are perhaps part of a large continent contiguous to America. On the old charts one finds such a shore line. There must have been some reason for this, although we do not know what it was. But experience teaches us that it is often necessary to go back to the opinions of the ancients."

The water between Gamaland and Siberia had been named

Anian, and Joseph went on: "If there is such a continent stretching out toward Kamchatka, it follows that the Strait of Anian would be located along the coast of Asia where Captain Bering sailed. Of course we do not know that there is an Anian Strait. But one cannot help feeling that somewhere between Asia and America there must be an important strait, whatever its character may be."

"But you have brought Kamchatka down to 45. Its southernmost point is above 51—about eleven minutes," said Bering.

"I saw that in your report. But Vries sighted this coast, which he calls Yesso, at 45."

"I don't know what Vries sighted. But I sailed around Kamchatka on my return to Okhotsk. I can give you my figures."

"It is quite possible that there is a strait here at 51." Joseph Delisle was speaking to himself rather than his guests. "That would make Yesso an island, as some believe it is."

Kossirefski had also been studying the map. "I have sailed through this Yesso, and it's all water," he said. "There are about eighteen small islands between Kamchatka and Japan. I've been on most of them. On the sixth one going south you find silver and there's a good anchorage there. On the one before the last there's a Japanese city."

Bering listened attentively. Kossirefski was grateful for the respect. "I can make you a good chart if you want it," he said to Bering.

"I would like it."

"That makes a difficult problem," said Joseph Delisle, taking up his charcoal. "Father Ignatius' islands probably lie east in the channel between Yesso and Gamaland. And I think I will draw the Kamchatka coast with a broken line, to show that it is a composite from conflicting sources."

Kossirefski smiled humbly. But Bering was indignant. "You can't combine my findings with Vries'. They don't combine! They're contradictory. Vries never saw Kamchatka!"

Chirikov chuckled. Leaning across the table toward Bering, he said, "Your opinions were formed in Siberia!"

"The work of the cartographer is full of just such problems," said Joseph Delisle. "At one time my brother had conclusive evidence that California was an island and equally conclusive evidence that it was a peninsula. I suppose you would say that those ideas could not be combined. But my brother placed an inscription across the northern end of California and no one could say whether he had intended an island or a peninsula!"

The silence which followed this revelation of the map maker's art was broken at last by Kossirefski.

"And so you misled no one! An ingenious solution!"

The plans for the Great Kamchatka Expedition were completed in December 1732. The expedition of discovery now included a scientific investigation of a quarter of the northern hemisphere. The orders pertaining to the work at sea covered more than was to be accomplished by Cook, Vancouver, La Perouse, and a century of navigation. And the work to be done in Siberia, en route to the sea, would have staggered Soviet Russia two centuries later. Bering was expected to accomplish everything in six years.

Detachments of men began leaving for Siberia in February 1733, but Bering did not get away till April. He remained at his desk struggling with a mass of papers which grew larger every day.

Several members of the Academy were to accompany him. Together with their servants and assistants, they made a party of forty men. The scholars were supplied with quadrants, thermometers, nocturnals, astrolabes, and Gunther's chains. They were taking bodyguards, scientific assistants, surveyors, landscape painters, instrument makers, interpreters (speaking Greek and Chaldean), secretaries, enormous quantities of

artists' supplies and scientific apparatus, and a library of several
hundred volumes. The other necessities of the expedition—
ship supplies, provisions, horses, barges, and even labor—were
to be supplied by the Siberian towns.

Bering moved the papers on his desk aimlessly. They were
a maze of detail. To explore the American coast as far as the
Spanish possessions; to introduce cattle raising on the Pacific
coast of Siberia; to describe the country, making a study of
the natural resources, especially minerals; to build a dockyard;
to establish ironworks at Okhotsk; to procure provisions; to
build ships at Okhotsk, and not on Kamchatka; to furnish land
and river transportation; to make a detailed presentation of the
ethnology, colonization, and history of Siberia and America;
to establish salt works at Okhotsk, a distillery on Kamchatka,
a smelting furnace at Yakutsk; to erect lighthouses and magazines along the Arctic; to chart the old world from Archangel
to Japan; to chart the rivers of Siberia; to explore all harbors
and estuaries on both coasts; to establish elementary and nau-
tical schools . . . A subexpedition to China had been ruled
out.

Bering thought of the seven hundred miles from Yakutsk
to Okhotsk without a single inhabitant. "Am I to establish
schools only where they are needed or everywhere?" But
the thought of those mountain passes reminded him that somewhere among the papers was an order to maintain mail service
between Moscow and Kamchatka and to the Chinese border,
with the necessities for mail service—men, horses, and roads—
all lacking.

The door of the study opened and Chirikov came across the
room. He was dressed in leather traveling clothes.

"I thought you left a month ago!" Bering said in surprise.

"I did. I'm halfway to Tobolsk now." Chirikov's manner,
like his clothes, was already Siberian. The uninhabited
stretches produced a good-natured lawlessness as certainly as

the frozen earth produced bog, and Bering accepted the one
as he did the other

"I came back to help the Academists get off. They were
received at court this morning, and there's a dinner for them
at Joseph Delisle's tonight. I thought you might like to go."

"I would like to go to Tobolsk, if I could get away from
these papers. Why should I want to go to Joseph Delisle's?"

The question was rhetorical, but Chirikov felt compelled to
say something in defense of the papers. "This expedition is
stupendous, isn't it? Nothing like it has ever been dreamed of
before!"

"It's not an expedition. It's a migration. It's a nightmare!"

Obviously the Commander was in no mood for company.
And Chirikov was. He moved toward the door. "We will
leave the first thing in the morning, sir."

"The gentlemen of the Academy won't be sober enough to
leave, for a week."

Bering left his desk and began to pace the room. He was in
agony, torn between his scrupulous honesty and his driving
desire to return to the Pacific. To sail those seas, to find America and Japan—how could he put aside that dream? And yet if
he could see no way to carry out his instructions, what right
had he to head the expedition to Siberia? He should resign
from this work if he did not expect to accomplish it.

"Only a fool could accept such orders," he groaned.

And then, so vividly that he thought he heard it with his
outward ear, came a clear, quiet voice: "Cross Siberia and
build a boat. . ... Ask the inhabitants the name of the place."

Bering stopped his pacing. Had he not sworn an oath to a
dying man? Suddenly he saw his yearning for the uncharted
seas, the unfinished work, as the binding force of a vow. And
at the same time he saw himself still under orders from the old
czar. A weight had fallen from him.

With a clear mind and an easy conscience Bering turned

back to his desk and took up an account of the things which
Pissarjev had accomplished to date. It was a rewriting of orders
sent in May 1731 and now looked on by the Senate as accomplished fact. To take Russians and Tungus and settle them in
the neighborhood of Okhotsk—Russians were now cultivating
the soil; the Tungus were tending herds of cattle; there were
flocks of fat sheep—to pick up at Yakutsk three hundred
young and strong men in prison for debt; to take from Russia
carpenters to build four or six ships; ironworkers to smelt
iron . . .

Bering laughed. "Perhaps he has done those things," he
said, remembering Pissarjev and remembering Yakutsk, a town
of five hundred, most of them too young and strong to be im-
prisonable for any cause. But the Senate was satisfied. And
there in Pissarjev's report were the cattle and the ironworks he
had just been worrying about. Why not the salt mines too?
There were many things which could safely be left to men
who would never do them. And Bering began to sort the work.

What would have to be taken care of by himself stood out
clearly enough. He must transport the whole cumbersome
expedition across Siberia. He would send parties north along
the rivers to explore the Arctic. From Okhotsk an expedition
would go south to Japan. He would put Spanberg in charge
of that. He himself would sail to America with Chirikov second in command. They could count on two hundred barrels of
whale meat from Kamchatka . . .

The party at Joseph Delisle's, scheduled for the evening,
had begun at noon immediately following the reception at
court. Chirikov found the guests standing among the loaded
wagons with their glasses of vodka and heard their excited
voices in the servants' quarters beyond. He made his way to
the study. The sumptuous room was unrecognizable in its
disorder. Rich draperies had been torn from their hangings;

slender gilt chairs had been overturned and broken. A dinner
had been served unnoticed and eaten unnoticed. Food was
scattered about on the rugs and cushions. Tense with self-
importance and the excitement of leaving for Siberia, it had
taken very little to make all the Academists drunk.

George Steller drank heavily, often to the point of insensi-
bility. As he drank he talked more and tolerated interruption
less, but there was no other change in his manner. His was the
first voice Chirikov heard as he entered the room. He was
talking about the natives of Kamchatka.

"It is necessary to remember that these men are not Chris-
tians. They are under the natural law. They leave their dead
to be devoured by beasts or, among some tribes, burn the
bodies. But we cannot say whether this is a sin or not in their
condition. I would like to know how universal the observance
is, whether or not some individuals show a natural reluctance
to follow these practices. And I would like to know what
attitude the tribe takes to this."

A boy was listening wide-eyed, completely unaware that
he had taken a smoked fish from the table and was chewing it
ravenously. With each phrase of Steller's he was composing
whole essays in natural theology.

Louis Delisle put his arm on Chirikov's shoulder and led
him to the table. "Drink fast," he said, "before this gets too
much for you. It got too much for Joseph a long time ago."

In two years Chirikov had come to know the Academists
better. He had learned how young they really were; most of
them were in their early twenties, and he was in his thirties. He
had learned that they did not have to be understood; one
could join their excitement and enjoy their company without
caring what they were talking about. He had learned these
things from Louis Delisle. Louis was his own age; like himself,
he knew nothing about the sciences and had been trained
primarily in the art of good fellowship.

Chirikov had been welcomed by the Academists. His advice to follow the coast of Siberia west had been written in the log of the St. Gabriel, and the scholars had admired him for it. He alone had understood what was required of a great expedition; he had shown himself an educated, civilized man among a lot of sailors. The Academists, on the other hand, were patronizing in their attitude toward Louis Delisle. He had wit, but no one except Joseph supposed he had any ability. Chirikov took his opinions ready formed and felt vaguely superior to Louis himself. And yet without Louis these gatherings would have had no charm for him. It was Louis's company he was seeking. Louis Delisle was so sure—sure in his laughter and in his indifference.

Chirikov was glad to be in this company again, to enjoy the high spirits, the excitement, and the talk. He drank fast, and soon the excitement of the room was surging through him too. He forgot the vandalism around him and felt only a deep love for his wonderful friends. The details of that evening were soon blurred, but a memory of the excitement, the hopes, the glory, and the intense brotherly love remained forever, keeping its sunset colors through all the dark years of Siberia.

For a moment he remembered the carts on the road to Tobolsk, and the backbreaking labor. It was for this! This gave the glory and the meaning to such work.

"This is the leaven!" he shouted, seizing George Steller by the shoulder. "The leaven of life!"

Steller had been drinking all day. He glanced around to place the "this." "Thought? You mean that thought is the leaven of life?" But Chirikov did not know what he meant. "Perhaps you mean drunkenness? Wine is the leaven of life. Drink to wine!"

Chirikov heard the historian, Gerhard Muller, shouting above the voices around him. He was discussing the easternmost point of Siberia, saying that Bering had not gone that far,

that he had turned back before he reached it. Chirikov made
his way toward him. He had been there; he ought to have
something to say. Suddenly he remembered it vividly. He felt
again the cold quiet of an hour five years before; he saw the
headland standing out across the water. No, by God! there
was nothing about it which proved that it was the easternmost
point of Siberia. Beyond, a waste of mist and water. And who
knew what lay in that mist? Not he, who had looked into
it. But Muller had other ways of knowing.

"I think you're right. Yes, by God! I'm sure you're right!"
Chirikov was glad to be agreeing with people.

"You've proved it, Muller. Shut up!" Johann Gmelin, the
chemist, was tired of the argument. He jumped onto the
table and held up his glass.

"To the new Russia! You over there, fill your glasses. We're
going to drink to the new Russia—true child of Peter the
Wonder-worker, to whom nothing is impossible, nothing too
great to attempt. Who but the children of Peter would have
dared plan the work which lies ahead of us today?"

Chirikov reeled against the table. His head swam with lighthouses, dockyards, salt mines, smelteries, ethnological reports,
geological reports, astronomical reports. Into this whirling
confusion had suddenly been injected the old czar! His stomach turned dangerously under the impact. Gmelin was making
a mistake about Peter, an important mistake, and Chirikov was
drunkenly determined to explain it.

"You are wrong about Peter!"

"Are you going to drink or aren't you?"

"I'll drink to Russia." He drained his glass. "But you're
wrong about Peter. You, Muller! You're a historian. You
ought to be interested in this!"

But the last drink had its effect, and Chirikov forgot what
it was he was interested in.

5. YAKUTSK

THE LITTLE VILLAGE of Yakutsk had been unable to shelter Bering's previous expedition on its way to the sea in 1726, and in 1735 the Great Kamchatka Expedition, numbering a thousand men, began to pour in. There had been advance notices from the Senate with orders to provide shelter and food—to assemble herds of cattle, to plant grain, and generally to make ready for them. But the orders of the Senate had not changed the natural resources of the country or altered the character of the people. Bering found Yakutsk the same dreary village it had been nine years before. There was no food, no quarters, and no preparation of any kind.

By the first fall a number of log buildings had been put up, but these were mostly warehouses. The men, faced with sleeping in the open, followed the custom of the natives and built themselves shelters of sod. By the first winter these earth buildings surrounded Yakutsk for several miles, and as month followed month the settlement grew steadily larger. Siberian exiles and natives were employed for additional labor, and at one time Bering had two thousand men working for him in Eastern Siberia. As time passed and the prospects of leaving Yakutsk grew fainter members of the expedition sent back to Russia for their wives and children.

Bering was held here for three years while he assembled supplies for the voyages to America and Japan and transported them to the sea. A high mountain range lies between Yakutsk and Okhotsk, and the transportation was chiefly by water. Barges were built at Yakutsk and warehouses put up along the route. The streams were swift and shallow. In the high mountains the men worked under the extremes of hot days and biting cold nights. They climbed along slippery banks, tugging the flat-bottomed boats upstream. In the Yudoma the current was so strong that it required thirty men to move a boat, the men working in water up to their waists and practically carrying the barges.

The men who did this work came into Yakutsk to spend their pay, and drinking houses sprang up everyplace in open violation of the law. Laughing native women and brawling men, Academist, exile, and fur trader, milled between the houses, grinding the narrow streets to mud which was frequently knee deep.

Gerhard Muller was established at the governor's house. He spent his time working in the archives, studying the reports of traders and tax collectors, to discover what was known about the East Cape of Siberia.

The Siberian trader seldom knew where he had been; his reports were chiefly an account of his courage and sufferings and of the cupidity of his companions. Among the litter of ignorance and irrelevancies on record at Yakutsk, the reports of Ivan Kossirefski were outstanding. This man, a fur trader, hiding under the robes of a monk, a robber and a cutthroat like his brother traders, was unique in that he always knew where he had been, and had actually been the places he said he had. But this uniqueness was not obvious to Gerhard Muller, or to any other scholar in the eighteenth century. The Academists had taken with them to Siberia, as recent works of travel, *The Voyage of Lemuel Gulliver* and *The Autobiography of Robinson Crusoe*, and they were looking for documents which were equally interesting and instructive. Moreover, Kossirefski was a contemporary and Gerhard Muller was a historian, interested in the oldest records he could find.

One evening in the winter of 1736 Muller and half a dozen of his friends sat in the library of the governor's house, facing the Commander. Muller had made a startling discovery and had sent a message to Bering asking him to come at once on a matter which required his immediate attention. A map of Muller's own making lay on the table before them. The Academists lolled comfortably in their chairs and watched the Commander, a stout man who sat stiffly with his hands on his knees. They noticed that he was short of breath. What Muller was about to tell was news only to Bering. The others had been over it many times.

Muller had before him a document which was almost a hundred years old, the report of one Semeon Deshnev. Deshnev had written with difficulty and had been proud to write at all. Muller had had difficulty in deciphering the hand and was proud to have read it at all. He picked up his paper nervously.

"I think I had better begin by simply reading you this report which I have found. You will notice that it is dated 1648."

Muller read slowly, for he felt that the words were momentous ones. "In the year 1648, June 20, I, Semeon, was sent from the Kolyma River to the Anadyr to find new, non-tribute-paying peoples. And in the year 1648, September 20, in going from the Kolyma to the sea, at a place where we stopped, the Chukchi in a fight wounded the trader, Gerasim. We were cold and hungry and naked and barefooted, and I, poor Semeon, and my companions went to the Anadyr in exactly ten weeks. We were unable to catch fish, there was no wood, and on account of hunger we separated. In the year 1654, in a fight, I captured from the Koriaks a Yakut woman belonging to Gerasim, and she said that Gerasim died of scurvy, some of his companions were killed, and the few who remained escaped in boats with their lives and she did not

know what became of them. And I, your servant, was left
with twenty-four men and with these companions suffered
cold, hunger, and want of other necessities before reaching
the Anadyr. On the way twelve men disappeared without our
knowing what became of them. And I reached the Anadyr
with twelve men and with these, not wishing to die of hunger,
went to fight against the Kanauli and Chodinski. These people resisted stubbornly and were soon destroyed."

Muller put down his paper and looked at the Commander in
silence. Realizing that something was expected of him, Bering
said:

"That was a hundred years ago?"

"Yes!" Muller said emphatically. "And do you see what
Deshnev did? He followed the coast from the mouth of the
Kolyma to the Eastern Sea!"

"Did he say that? Did he say he followed the coast?" Bering asked in surprise.

"He does not say 'coast.' But he says he went from the
Kolyma to the sea, and it is quite obvious what he means. He
says the journey took exactly ten weeks. No mention is made
of ice obstructions, so we may assume there were none."

Bering was unable to follow the argument. Feeling that the
reasonings of these men were beyond his abilities, he made no
attempt to weigh them but sat waiting to hear the conclusion.

"And so you see," Muller went on, "what your expedition
in 1728 failed to establish—namely that there is a sea route over
the north of Siberia, and therefore that Asia and America are
separate continents—I have been able to prove from the records here in Yakutsk."

Muller could no longer endure the dull face of the Commander, which did not lighten with interest. He said angrily,
"I thought you would be interested to know that the question
has been settled. At least you can understand my satisfaction
in the matter."

Bering roused himself. "I am interested! I am very glad to know that you have settled the question to your satisfaction. . . . Was this what you wanted to tell me?"

"That is in essence what I wanted to tell you," Muller said. "I have a map here which I have drawn according to this and some other reports which I have found. It differs in some respects from the chart you made in '28. If you are interested in considering these differences, I can explain to you in each case what I have based my decisions on."

The young men moved closer to the table, to follow the argument as Bering defended his chart against Muller's well-prepared criticisms. But Bering did not understand the eagerness around him. He got stiffly to his feet.

"Those are matters for you to decide, gentlemen. I must go back to my work."

He left the table without another word. Halfway across the room he remembered that this was not a company of sailors and turned. "A good evening to you."

When the door had closed behind him the Academists looked at one another and laughed.

"His work! What does the old boy do with his time?"

"He took it calmly enough," someone said.

"Why should he care one way or the other? He has a comfortable life—authority, position, and nothing to do. Why should he trouble himself about geography?"

Muller was examining his map. "Look at this!" he cried. "Come look at this!" He was pointing to a cape he had drawn north of Kamchatka but far south of the Arctic. "That is Captain Bering's East Cape! It agrees in every detail! So—in '28 he wasn't as far north as he thought, by a full six degrees."

Bering walked home alone through the noisy streets of Yakutsk. Pitch torches burned before the principal buildings and lighted up the faces in the crowd. Drunken men, seeing the familiar figure of the Commander, made way for him with a respect that was unmixed with fear.

Coming into his own room, he found George Steller waiting for him. A look of surprise and annoyance crossed his face.

"What is it you want?" he asked.

Steller had been pacing the room nervously. "I have come to ask you to do something about the conditions in this town," he said. "As you know, three men have been stabbed to death in Yakutsk within the last week, and no investigations are being made."

"You should discuss that with the governor. I do not represent the law."

"The governor is an incompetent, provincial official——"

The door of a tavern opposite was thrown open, and Steller's words were drowned in the shoutings of men who stumbled across the narrow street and lurched against the cabin walls.

"Do you suppose that tavern has a license to distill liquor? That one, or any of the others?" Steller asked when the noise had subsided.

"I don't know whether they have or not," Bering answered. "If St. Petersburg is interested in maintaining law in Yakutsk, they can send soldiers to maintain it. That is not my business."

"What is your business, may I ask?"

"To explore the seas between Asia and America! And so long as the barges move I am not interested in anything else."

The answer had seemed obvious enough to Bering, but to Steller, immersed in the problems of Yakutsk, it seemed a witticism, or an evasion. He turned on his heel and left the room.

Bering sat down at his desk. It was covered with letters from St. Petersburg that he had not found time to answer. The noises of the street rang in his ears. There were too many people in Yakutsk. With a quarter that number he could have gotten ahead. And there were too many letters to write. He rested his head on his arm and in a few minutes was sleeping with his face in the papers.

Mail service was maintained between Yakutsk and St. Petersburg, and it carried chiefly complaints and recrimination and slander. There were numerous letters from unofficial sources informing the Senate that Bering was interested only in his salary, that he took bribes, and that he was making a fortune out of traffic in liquor and women. These crimes seemed only human and alarmed no one.

But the provincial authorities made more serious charges. They complained of waste of money and lack of discipline. The materials which Bering assembled out of an unknown, unpopulated country seem nothing short of the miracle of loaves and fishes. But the reports stated that he was fond of show, did everything at enormous expense, and did not know how to avail himself of what was at hand. Moreover, in his conduct toward his men, the reports continued, he was timid, hesitant, and lenient—not the type of man to head a great enterprise in such a barbaric country as Eastern Siberia. This was a serious charge. The Senate wrote Bering, threatening to fine him, court-martial him, reduce his rank, if he did not change his ways.

During the three years spent at Yakutsk many letters passed between Bering and the Admiralty.

CAPTAIN BERING TO THE ADMIRALTY COLLEGE:

It is not possible for me to go to Okhotsk with my men until I have sent some provisions ahead. Otherwise I would take the risk of starving them to death, putting an end to all hopes of accomplishing anything, and thus incur a heavy responsibility. Some of my men must remain at Yakutsk in charge of the affairs of the expedition there, and to forward provisions. Others will remain at the Maya harbor, Yudoma Cross, and at the Urak landing to guard the magazines and attend to the transportation of necessaries to Okhotsk, for it is not yet possible to feed so many people there. Trees and grass do not grow there and are not found in the vicinity on account of the gravel.

THE ADMIRALTY COLLEGE TO CAPTAIN BERING:

Your expedition is a very protracted one and apparently it is being conducted somewhat carelessly on your part, which is shown by the fact that it has taken nearly two years to reach Yakutsk. Moreover, it appears from your report that your stay in Yakutsk will be long; in fact there seems to be no reason to hope that you will succeed in getting any further. As a consequence of all this the Admiralty is extremely dissatisfied with your arrangements and will not let matters go on without an investigation. If in the future any negligence whatsoever occurs, an investigation will be instituted against you for insubordination and for negligence in an affair of state.

CAPTAIN BERING TO THE ADMIRALTY COLLEGE:

Prior to our arrival in Yakutsk not a single pood of provisions had been sent to Okhotsk, not a single vessel had been built for transporting these provisions and supplies. No laborers were to be had and no arrangements had been made by the Siberian government officials, notwithstanding the fact that an imperial ukase had ordered these things. We have done all this. We built transports. At the stopping places on the Maya, at the mouth of the Yudoma, at the Cross, and on the Urak, we erected magazines and dwellings for the forces and also built four winter huts between Yudoma Cross and the Urak as places of refuge during the winter.

Notwithstanding the fact that the authorities were directed to prepare food for the expedition, nothing whatever was done in this regard; but on the contrary they monopolized the

supplies of the Tungus who furnished my first expedition
with an abundance of fish and upon whom I had depended. It
is quite impossible to get anything in the way of food except
the legal military provisions consisting of flour and groats.
For this reason we are forced to give the men leave of absence
in the summer so that they may obtain food by fishing, thus
causing a loss of time and neglect of the work of the expedi-
tion.

    From the government officer in Okhotsk, Gregory Pissar-
jev, we have not, since the day of our arrival here up to the
present time, received the slightest assistance in transportation,
shipbuilding, or anything else whatsoever. Nor have we any
hope of obtaining any such assistance in the future, for he has
sent me a written notification refusing to assist in the trans-
portation.

    The following year the Imperial Cabinet asked the Admir-
alty to look into the Kamchatka Expedition and see if it could
not be brought to a head. The Admiralty's device for bringing
the expedition to a head was to cut Bering's salary.

THE ADMIRALTY COLLEGE TO CAPTAIN BERING:
    Inasmuch as you, in spite of the express orders of the Ad-
miralty, wherein it is stated that your expedition is protracted
and is carelessly conducted, have not reported to the Admi-
ralty the cause of your delay, and say nothing about when you
intend to leave Yakutsk, you are hereby deprived of your
supplemental salary until you continue on the expedition
which has been entrusted to you.

    The tavern Steller had spoken about was filled with noisy
men crowded around a large table in the center of the room. In
the shadow of the walls Chirikov and Louis Delisle were sitting with Dimitri Ovtsin, who had returned in disgrace from
an expedition to the Arctic.

While crossing Siberia, Bering had sent a number of expeditions north along the rivers to chart sections of the Arctic coast. In each case the officers in command had run foul of the local authorities, who made charges against them to St. Petersburg. In each case the Senate had believed the charges and recalled and punished the officers without regard for the work they were doing. Of all the men sent to the Arctic, Ovtsin was the only one who finished his work. But he too had been recalled and reduced to the rank of sailor because it was reported that he had gotten in touch with the wife of an exiled Dolgoruk. The Dolgoruks had fallen so recently, and from such a height, that the mere name terrorized the Senate. To be reinstated Ovtsin would have to serve as a sailor and be recommended for promotion, and he had come to Bering for this. But there were no voyages to send him on.

Another expedition, under Lassenius, had left Yakutsk the previous year to follow the coast from the mouth of the Kolyma to the sea. Lassenius had been caught by the ice in mid-August but, being near shore, with ample provisions and timber for building, decided to winter where he was. By November seventeenth the polar night had begun, and two days later, on the nineteenth, every man in the crew was stricken with a sudden, violent form of scurvy. Three men made their way down to Yakutsk and a relief party was sent for the others. But the relief had arrived too late. Men from the Lassenius relief were now back in Yakutsk, telling their story in all the drinking houses.

"Lassenius was spared an investigation. It was all for the best," Ovtsin said bitterly.

Chirikov and Delisle had heard Ovtsin's complaints too often and were tired of them. They made no answer but sat watching the men in the center of the room.

A sailor from the Lassenius relief was standing on a barrel and shouting, "What did we find? We found thirty frozen bodies. That's what we found. Is that the sort of thing you send a relief for?"

"Did you bring them back?" someone asked.

The sailor caught sight of the officers watching him and got down from the barrel. They saw him pushing his way through the crowd.

"He seems to know us. Is he a friend of yours, Ovtsin?" Delisle asked.

The sailor sat down with them. "Captain Chirikov? I was with you on the *St. Gabriel*."

Chirikov did not remember, but he answered cordially, "Oh yes. You were on Kamchatka. Yes."

A silence followed. Delisle saw that the man had something he wanted to say and handed him the bottle of brandy. The sailor took a small drink to acknowledge the courtesy. Then, in a lowered voice, he told them the secret thing he had not been able to tell anyone else.

"Lassenius' men. They had built a barracks. A good, tight building. There was fuel there that they hadn't burned. And they had provisions for two years."

They had all that men need. And yet they had died. Delisle leaned forward in interest. "What killed them?"

The man's eyes grew round with terror. "It was the dark. A man can't live in that dark," he whispered.

The four men sat in cold silence. They saw the polar night capping the world with horror. Its dark vapors seeped through the dimly lighted tavern. Chirikov remembered that he had once wanted to winter in that shadow. He stood up quickly and pulled Delisle to his feet.

"Come on. Let's go where they have lights."

In the nature of things, the Great Kamchatka Expedition should have settled down at Yakutsk and written reports on America from there. That it did not was due entirely to Vitus

Bering. Against the will of every man in Yakutsk, politicians, Academists, and laborers, the great glacier moved on toward the sea. And the force which moved it was the determination of one man, working under orders from a dead leader.

Bering had natural difficulties to contend with—mountains and forests and shallow streams, the long northern winter, and the scarcity of food in Eastern Siberia. But the largest factor in holding the expedition at Yakutsk for three years was the Academy.

From Yakutsk the Academists made expeditions to various parts of Siberia and brought back reports, some of which were valuable. But these excursions did not help move the supplies toward Okhotsk, and Bering equipped and manned each one of them. The scholars refused to have their work hampered by physical discomfort. They would not walk, they would not ride on barges, and they took with them everywhere the standards and the luxuries of Europe. Another captain burdened by such scholars called them "damned disturbers of the peace" and threatened to maroon them. But Bering said nothing. For five years he built them cabin boats, supplied them with horses, transported their wines and changes of clothing, and sent relief expeditions for them when they were lost.

Only after three years at Yakutsk, when the whole expedition threatened to sink under its enormous weight, did Bering's patience give out. He then refused to build any more cabin boats or make any better provision for the scientists than was made for the other members of the expedition. On the road to Okhotsk they would have to travel as other men traveled, eat as other men ate.

The scholars did not go on. Only George Steller and Louis Delisle reached Kamchatka and America. The others returned to Russia, talking about passive resistance. But they had left their mark on the expedition. Their ideas still influ-

enced the actions of the Senate. Bering was still under orders
to sail by Joseph Delisle's map and to look for Gamaland. But
their mark lay most heavily in the wasted years and the wasted
strength. Bering had now passed his prime and was worn out
by frustrations and futile bickerings.

6. OKHOTSK

SPANBERG had been at Okhotsk three years when Bering
arrived. Here on a sandspit, in flat, treeless country and cold,
raw fog, Spanberg had built a city—dockyards, magazines,
barracks, houses for the officers, and churches. The harbor
was filled with ships which needed only provisions to go to
sea. He had built the *Archangel Michael* and the *Hope* for
his own voyage to Japan, he had repaired the *St. Gabriel* and
the *Fortune* for Bering's use, and had constructed numerous
small ferrying boats. To build these ships, Spanberg's men had
floated timber for twenty miles and had brought pitch pine
from Kamchatka. For the buildings they had hauled the clay
and baked the tiles. They had carried the wood which they
burned for charcoal three or four miles and their drinking
water two miles.

Crossing the flat plains toward Okhotsk, Bering could see
that this post was not as he had left it. Coming nearer, he made
out two stockaded villages instead of one and saw a horseman
coming toward them from the nearer village. It was a messenger from Pissarjev demanding that Captain Bering come at
once to the governor.

"Why are there two villages?" Bering asked.

"Captain Spanberg has his place and the governor has his,"

the messenger explained. But on the long ride back to Okhotsk he had nothing more to say.

This time Bering was not kept waiting. He was taken at once to the governor's hall—a long, low-ceilinged room littered with guns, clothing, and trash of every kind, and unspeakably filthy. Pissarjev was there, sitting in a chair by the window and wrapped in shawls. He did not get up or make any apology for it.

He began speaking at once. "Captain Bering? I want to tell you about your man. He sells the military rations and gives the men half their allowance. He has manufactured twice the amount of brandy shown in his report. And he is in communication with the Dolgoruks! You think I wouldn't know that. But I have my ways of knowing."

Bering was too shocked by the change in Pissarjev to attend to what he was saying, and it was several minutes before he understood that he was speaking of Spanberg. It was ten years since Bering had seen this man in Kamchatka. He had been an old man then, and vicious—but a strong old man, and Bering had supposed that nothing could change that. But this thing, huddled in its shawls, was merely the venom that had been in Pissarjev; everything else—the strength, the pride, and the wit—had been eaten away. And that was the ravage of ten years in Siberia!

"He is less a man than a monkey!" Bering told himself.

"Oh, I can tell you," Pissarjev went on, "he has become a captain without losing any of the tricks of a sailor. The natives say he must be either a general incognito or an escaped convict." A laugh flickered in Pissarjev's eyes but disappeared immediately under a weak, knowing smile. He leaned forward confidentially.

"Shall I tell you the latest thing he has done? He has erected a monument to a bear!" Bering thought Spanberg was being accused of idolatry, but the old man went on: "He claims that he killed it himself with a knife. He did no such thing! I have my men there—I know! That bear was killed by a Tungus. I have reported the whole business to St. Petersburg and there will be an investigation!"

When Bering left Pissarjev's hall a feeling of horror and fright had settled over him. Pissarjev's charges seemed too absurd to be listened to, even in St. Petersburg. But in the man himself Bering had seen the terrible fact of time. He rode toward the sea, thinking that he too had spent ten years in Siberia. He remembered the czar lying in his bed. Peter had given this work to a man of forty-five, and it was now in the hands of a man nearing sixty. He had reached the sea at last and was ready to begin—and who could say how much time remained to him before the hand should tremble and bad luck defeat him?

Coming into Spanberg's town, he saw the wooden figure of the bear. It stood on a plot of ground set aside for it. Bering stopped his horse. Around him were the barracks and the warehouses and beyond lay the ships—necessary work, well done. And at the center a decoration, a pathetic boast that even here man's strength was greater than his needs. Bering softened toward Spanberg. He would not ask him to remove the statue.

But he took him to task for the trouble with Pissarjev. "Why do you harass that old man?" he demanded. "You know he's the governor here and we have to live under him."

"It's impossible to live under him. He's a foulmouthed, poisonous old babbler. Moreover, he's dangerous."

"He's senile and you aren't!" Bering spoke sharply. "Find some way to get along with him!"

Spanberg understood an order. "Very well. But I wish I'd done away with him before you got here."

Okhotsk was as cosmopolitan a port as any in the world. Koriaks and Russians predominated; Germans, Finns, Danes,

Swedes, French, and English were there in numbers. But there were no Japanese. Bering had explicit orders from the Senate to find shipwrecked Japanese to put aboard the *Archangel Michael* and return to their own country. The Senate expected the people of Japan to believe that Spanberg's expedition had been gotten up for this charitable purpose, and not as a scouting party. However, if the Japanese government refused to accept its nationals, the order went on, they were not to be brought back to Kamchatka, but marooned on some convenient island. But there were no Japanese to repatriate, or maroon, and Spanberg sailed out of Okhotsk without an excuse for his voyage. He was carrying provisions for two years.

When Spanberg had gone, building was begun on the ships for America, the *St. Peter* and the *St. Paul*. Again the labor—pitch brought from Kamchatka, timber floated twenty miles—altogether two years' work to build two ships measuring eighty by twenty by nine feet. Bering made up the crews, seventy-five men to each ship. He signed Ovtsin, who had been degraded for his work in the Arctic, for the *St. Peter*. Bering himself was to be in command of the *St. Peter*, and he was taking with him one naval lieutenant, a Swede, Sven Waxel. Chirikov, who was to be in command of the *St. Paul*, was taking three lieutenants and the astronomer, Louis Delisle. But Bering probably considered the lists equal—he had Ovtsin as a sailor, and for mate he had the seventy-year-old Esselberg who had sailed all the seas of the world. At the last minute Bering realized that he had no scientist on board and sent a messenger to find George Steller.

The ships were built at Okhotsk, by order of the Senate. But the expedition was to sail from the eastern coast of Kamchatka, and it was necessary to have a port there. During the summer of 1738 Elagin, navigator for Chirikov's ship, was sent to look for a harbor. He found Avacha Bay near the southern end of the peninsula and built Petropavlovsk, the Harbor of St. Peter and St. Paul. But the freight packets were not seaworthy and the supplies for the American voyage had to be ferried to the west coast of Kamchatka and taken to Elagin by the overland route.

Spanberg returned after fifteen months. When his ships appeared in the harbor the town rang with excitement. And as the men began coming ashore the excitement grew. Spanberg had succeeded in everything!

He spread out his maps before Bering. "Kossirefski said there were eighteen islands. There are thirty-one! And I've got them all—in spite of fog every day. Fog so thick you couldn't see shore thirty feet away!"

Spanberg had moved through this fog, along a chain of submerged volcanoes whose steep sides gave no anchorage, and had charted the thirty-one islands of the Kurils. But he had done more. He had continued south, sailing beyond the fog out into clear blue water. He had sailed along rich, cultivated shores covered with vineyards and orange trees. Here and there were villages. The people of the villages had gathered on the shore to look at the strange ships and at night had lighted beacons to guide them. South of 37 Spanberg had dropped anchor before a large city. Great dignitaries had come out to the ship, men of high rank with nothing to sell. They brought gifts of wine and sweets. Spanberg had given them brandy and they had enjoyed it. He had shown them his chart and they had understood it. They had pointed out the place where the ships lay and had said "Nippon."

The Japanese had known the islands north of them. "They say that there are islands, one close to the other, all the way to America. They say these islands, and America itself, have always been a place of refuge for their people."

Spanberg had asked other questions about geography and they had answered them all courteously and at great length, but as there had been no interpreter he had not understood what they said.

But he had still more news. From Japan he had sailed out to sea and had returned to Kamchatka over the Gamaland shown on Joseph Delisle's map. It was not there. There was nothing there but open sea.

The meanest laborer in Okhotsk understood all that Spanberg had accomplished, and the town went wild celebrating his success. The excitement was so great that someone went to Kamchatka to tell Elagin's men. Reports were sent to St. Petersburg, and the Admiralty enthusiastically gave out the good news to the world, taking care, however, to misstate all the facts so that no other nation should profit by these discoveries. The czarina sent a personal note to Spanberg congratulating him on his success and ordering him to come to her at once.

But the joy was to be short-lived, and Spanberg's good work had to wait on posterity for its vindication. Governor Pissarjev also made a report. He secretly warned the Admiralty that Spanberg had not gone to Japan at all. This seemed probable to the Admiralty, especially as Spanberg had not found Japan where it was shown on their maps.

A few days beyond Yakutsk, on his way to Russia, Spanberg was met by a messenger with an order from the Senate, telling him that he had not been to Japan and ordering him to go at once. He returned to Okhotsk too angry a man to be fit for work. Bering reprovisioned the *Archangel Michael* and the *Hope* out of his own supplies, and Spanberg sailed again.

Barely six months later his ships reappeared in the harbor. Spanberg showed his maps—the maps of the first voyage, without a correction. Bering looked at them and could make no comment; the man's anger was too great for him.

"You are doing a very dangerous thing," he said at last.

"I'm going to take these maps to St. Petersburg and see who it is says I haven't been to Japan."

"You can't do that. It's treason to leave Siberia without orders."

"Then I will commit treason. But I will not make that expedition to Japan again!"

Spanberg had gone. Spanberg, the only man in Siberia that Bering really understood, the only man he had ever really relied upon. And he had gone to certain arrest and imprisonment. The raw fog bit into men's spirits. They began to have trouble with the natives. The Koriaks, who had carried freight for six years, refused to carry any more. The Russians resorted to guns to keep them at their work and the Koriaks discovered sabotage. Provisions which had been assembled at enormous labor were stolen, lost, burned, and abandoned.

Bering stood at a window, looking out at the tidy town and the well-built houses. Spanberg's work. A few more packets to Kamchatka, and it would be abandoned, left to the fog and Pissarjev. The *St. Gabriel* was moving out of harbor with Chirikov in command. While Bering watched she struck a sandbank and keeled. He remembered that she was carrying the supply of biscuit for the American voyage and turned from the window. He did not want to see what became of her.

When Chirikov came in several hours later Bering was sitting at his desk with no work before him.

"That bar was on Kossirefski's map," he said without emotion.

"Yes, it was." Chirikov, too, was tired to the breaking point.

"How much of the biscuit did you save?"

Chirikov answered with a forced indifference, "Less than a quarter, I should say."

7. PETROPAVLOVSK

IT WAS mid-May at the harbor of St. Peter and St. Paul. A gloomy gray sky and a cold wind flecked with snow. The two ships for America stood in the snow-covered ice of the bay, and a dozen log buildings lined the beach. Sofron Khitrov, a giant, red-bearded Cossack, leaned against the wall of the smithy watching the men loading water casks onto the *St. Peter*. The watch which was just going off straggled across the ice to the bathhouse on the opposite bank. A small man, a stranger, was coming across the bay toward him.

"Are you the master of the *St. Peter?*" the stranger asked.

"I am."

"I am George Steller of the Imperial Academy. I am sailing with you, as mineralogist. When do you think the ships will leave?"

Khitrov turned his head and looked toward the hall by the church where the naval officers were gathered at that moment, to decide just that. But he knew the answer without waiting for a council of the officers. He waved his hand toward the bay.

"That ice will go out in a couple of weeks. We have clear water by the end of May. The sea is full of drift ice through July, but we will leave in June."

"You have drift ice in July?" The stranger was interested. "That must come from American rivers, and proves that America is not far from here. But how long do you navigators expect the voyage to last?"

Khitrov smiled. "That ice doesn't come from rivers. It

comes from the North Pole. But the voyage has to be short. We lost the sea biscuit in the harbor at Okhotsk."

"That biscuit!" The stranger spoke impatiently. "I've been here two days and I've heard about that biscuit two hundred times. It's of no consequence whatsoever. The natives of Kamchatka have never heard of grain and they are quite as healthy as you are. We can take dried fish instead of biscuit."

Khitrov's smile broadened. His white teeth showed above his red beard. He knew Professor Delisle, a gentleman who liked his drink and made no trouble for anyone. This man was different.

"You're telling me my men can go without bread? My men aren't Chukchi. They're Russians."

"I'm not a Chukchi either. But I've eaten nothing but native food for a year, and it nourishes me just as it does them."

"Each man can have his own opinion, I suppose," Khitrov said tolerantly.

"No indeed! My opinions are based on reason and experience, and yours are based on nothing at all."

Khitrov stooped to look at the man who spoke to him in this way. "I thought I knew all the kinds of men there were!" he said.

But the stranger had finished his conversation. He turned abruptly and walked away toward the ships.

Khitrov called after him. "You! Little fellow! That ice comes from the north!"

In the council hall the officers sat about a table, listening indifferently as the Commander reviewed what they all knew. The plans for a two-year voyage beginning this spring would have to be abandoned, due to the loss of the biscuit. They could, of course, wait and make that voyage next spring. He glanced around the table; there was a murmur of disapproval. That seemed unwise. It would be difficult to keep the men occupied, and the authorities at St. Petersburg were impatient. The alternative was a short voyage this summer to be followed by a longer one next year when the supplies for it could be ready.

"It is decided then that we will make a voyage this summer. In planning the voyage we must remember that these shores are unapproachable in the autumn gales, and arrange to return to this harbor during the last days of September."

The men straightened in their chairs as Bering went on to discuss the evidence of land lying near them to the north—his own observations and tales of natives and traders, stories of men who came from the sea wearing walrus ivory in their lips, who told of islands lying one beyond another, a day's sail apart.

"They say that on these islands are sable, beaver, deer, and all kinds of green trees. Although these reports cannot be trusted implicitly, I feel that they should be followed up and a voyage made in that direction."

Chirikov glanced around the table. "I think we are all agreed that America lies close to Siberia in the north," he said.

Bering understood this as a protest and waited for him to go on. He understood that Chirikov would speak for the Academists.

"We could not start north till the end of July, as that sea is full of ice. And therefore I feel we could use the time we have better by sailing south in search of Gamaland. This country is also said to have great wealth in gold and pearls, and surely those reports should be followed up too."

"The wealth that is said to be on Gamaland makes me doubt the reality of that country more than anything else I know about it," Bering answered. "So far we have had no evidence of land lying in that direction. And as you say, we are practically certain of land lying east and north of here. I would

like to establish that this summer, if only to have something
to report to the Admiralty."

The white-haired Esselberg got to his feet. "There is no
Gamaland," he said angrily. "And the Commander knows that
as well as I do. We have Spanberg's maps and Kossirefski's. It's a
sinful waste of God's time to go looking for it any further."

"We are under orders from the Senate to look for it,"
Chirikov said indignantly.

Louis Delisle had jumped to his feet. He did not have a
voice in this council, but his family's honor had been outraged.
"You have my brother Joseph's maps! Do you set more store
by the word of a couple of vagabonds than you do by the
work of Joseph Delisle?"

"Yes. I do."

"Esselberg!" Bering's voice rang out sharply and brought
the room to order. Esselberg sat down slowly. Would the
Commander dare tell him he was wrong?

"When we reach Gamaland we could follow the coast
north, and come around by the waters you want to investigate," Chirikov said, trying to ignore the interruption.

But Bering turned to the mate. "You and I are old men,
Esselberg. These others are young. You and I are foreigners
and they are native Russians. They must have a voice in this
undertaking. And if it is the wish of this council that we
should look for land south of here, that is what I will do. I
will say to you plainly that I do not believe any land lies in
that direction. But it is characteristic of old men to hold their
opinions too firmly. You and I might be wrong."

Chirikov was softened by the unexpected concession. "I do
not think we should spend much time looking for this land,"
he said. He took up a map. "It is shown here on the 47th
parallel. I suggest that we sail south by east as far as 46. If no
land is found by that time, we can change the course to east
by north steadily till land is discovered. By starting this voyage

in June we will probably reach the American coast sooner than if we waited till July to sail north. Are you willing to sail that course, Captain Commander?"

"Nothing is probable about things you know nothing about, Alexei Ivanovich. But since you are all determined on this, we will go in search of Gamaland as soon as the ice is out of the bay."

The officers sat back in their chairs. The question of the meeting had been decided. And the most unfortunate decision possible had been made. The Alaska Peninsula and the chain of islands that lead from America to Kamchatka sweep out in a curve that dips south of Petropavlovsk. By sailing east they would have found this land in a few days. But by first sailing to the 46th parallel in search of Gamaland they would pass three hundred miles south of these islands. Beginning the eastward voyage at this point, they would run parallel to the land for fifteen hundred miles without sighting anything.

Bering was now reading the general instructions for the voyage.

"If you should see land, fly both the flag and the jack and keep them flying until the other sees them and hoists his flag. . . .

"If, may God preserve us, the ship should run aground, lower all sails, hoist the jack, and keep on firing until you make sure that the others are aware of the danger. . . .

"If on the way we should become separated, we are to cruise for three days near the spot where we lost sight of each other. If during that time we should not find one another, from which misfortune may God preserve us, we are to sail the course agreed on. . . .

"If after separating we should be in a region where foreign vessels might be expected, in order to recognize one another we should fly a blue flag from the main topmast cross trees. . . ."

The officers had listened attentively. They agreed with one another that all the possible mishaps of the sea had been covered.

"It only remains for me to read you the Orders of the Senate."

The Orders of the Senate contrasted sharply with the general instructions for the voyage. As Bering passed from the small plans of sailors to the broad plans of statesmen his voice lost its decisive tone and he read slowly, not certain that he understood the full meaning of the words.

"Officers in command of ships at sea should keep secret the instructions of the Admiralty College. For this purpose special instructions are issued which may be made public. These instructions state that at the request of the St. Petersburg, Paris, and other academies, the Emperor Peter the Great sent, out of curiosity, an expedition along his own shores to determine whether Asia and America were united. But the expedition did not settle that point. Now Her Imperial Majesty, influenced by the same reasons, is ordering a similar expedition for a similar purpose. If you should come to settlements under European or Asiatic jurisdiction or if you should meet with ships of European or Asiatic governments, and are asked the object of your voyage, you may tell them what has just been said. If they demand to see your instructions, show them. This will allay their suspicions, because it is well known that European powers have sent out expeditions and that the question whether Asia and America are united is still unanswered. . . .

"On the voyage the two ships are to keep together, work together, and do all in their power to advance naval science. They are to examine the waters between Kamchatka and America. Search should be made for good harbors and for forests where timber for shipbuilding is to be had. Let mineralogists with a guard go ashore and prospect. If precious minerals are found, the governor at Okhotsk should be notified. . . . .

"If people are found they are to be treated kindly, they are to be given presents, they are to be asked the extent of their country and its resources, and they are to be invited to become our subjects and to pay tribute. If they are unwilling to do so they are to be let alone, and no time should be wasted in arguing with them. . . .

"Always be on your guard not to fall into a trap, and not to show the people you meet with the way to Kamchatka."

8. THE "ST. PETER" OUTWARD BOUND

THE *St. Peter* and *St. Paul* were towed out of the Harbor of the Holy Apostles and dropped anchor in the roadstead of Avacha Bay. Here they lay for a week. The wind blew steadily from the southeast, fair for America but contrary for Gamaland. When it shifted, toward evening on June fifteenth, it brought fog, but the *St. Peter* beat the drums and rang the bells to call the *St. Paul*, and together they put to sea. Following the custom of the sea, Bering isolated himself from the ship and kept to his cabin.

Going south, the ships passed out of the fog and for a week had fair weather—a blue sea and a blue sky and the wind behind them—a week of pleasant sailing to no profit. They reached the 46th parallel without sighting land. Then Bering from the *St. Peter* signaled the *St. Paul* to draw near. When the two ships were within calling distance his lieutenant, Sven Waxel, spoke through the trumpet.

"We have now sailed over the region where Gamaland is

supposed to be, and we see that it does not exist. We shall therefore set the course east by north for America."

The ships changed their course. As they moved north, Chirikov's ship, the *St. Paul*, began to fall behind the *St. Peter*. Three times the *St. Peter* took in sail and waited for her to come closer. Finally she fell so far astern that the *St. Peter* turned about and beat toward her. The Commander gave the trumpet to Master Khitrov.

"Ask them if they are still agreed to sail the northerly course, or if they want to look for Gamaland further."

Khitrov was exasperated by such sailing. He felt that the *St. Paul* needed a plain order. When she had come close enough he called his message.

"You are coming up south of the destination. Change your tack—if you are sailing the course agreed on."

Elagin called from the *St. Paul*, "It will be time for that when the wind changes. . . ." He was speaking against the wind and the words were lost. But the *St. Paul* had had an order from the Commander's vessel, and Khitrov saw no reason why he should have heard anything at all. He put away the trumpet and returned to his work.

At ten o'clock that night the *St. Paul* had again fallen behind and at eleven o'clock could not be seen. When the watch changed at one Khitrov learned that she had disappeared and laid to. At dawn he informed the Commander, and the *St. Peter*, following the instructions given at the council, turned into the wind and beat back to the place where she had last seen the *St. Paul*.

For three days they fought to remain in that sea, keeping a lookout at the topmast day and night. Bering himself came on deck frequently. As watch followed watch with nothing to report, his uneasiness increased, until at last the fear that the *St. Paul* was in trouble gave place to the realization that she had taken her own course.

The shock was almost too great for Bering, now in his sixties and weakened by hard work and poor food. The scurvy which had smoldered as a dull ache in his hands and feet suddenly flared through all his body

That Chirikov was impetuous and headstrong he knew. But this disregard for the fundamental laws of the sea was more than that—it was the irresponsibility of a child. With such a child for captain, the *St. Paul* was sailing an unknown sea, for an unknown coast—sailing to certain disaster. Bering called Khitrov.

"What did the *St. Paul* answer when you asked if they wanted to look further for Gamaland?"

"The words were lost on the wind. I believe they were agreed to sail for America, but thought the tack they were on would bring them around in time."

"You are not certain what they said?"

"No sir."

"Then set the course south. We will go as far as the 45th parallel. It is possible they misunderstood your message and have done just that."

The *St. Peter* turned south and kept that course for three days. Bering was too restless to remain in his cabin. No captain could lightly lose a ship and seventy-five men. And now that he was lost, Bering discovered that Chirikov meant more to him than a ship. This boy that Peter had given him to train, and whom he had not trained, had become his son.

Steller saw the Commander standing by the rail, scanning the horizon, and joined him. "I believe we have to conclude that this Gamaland is the invention of the map makers," he said cheerfully. "That these gentlemen are capable of committing such blunders is no surprise to me. A cartographer once asserted with all his might against me that Canton lies on the 45th parallel. And another informed me that the Maldive Islands lie in the Mediterranean Sea."

THE GREAT KAMCHATKA EXPEDITION 73

Bering turned on him in anguish. "We are looking for the *St. Paul*," he said.

When they had reached the 45th parallel without sighting Gamaland or the *St. Paul*, Bering gave orders to return to 46 and sail the course decided on in council. He then retired to his cabin and his bed, and the despondency which accompanies scurvy darkened around him.

For fifteen years Bering had drawn strength from the splendor of the work he had to do. And now the dream had faded. He could no longer feel its value. Instead of excitement and glory, he found himself alone on the seas with a dreary mission which had to be fulfilled. When the vision is lost, duty replaces enthusiasm and the strength of a man is put to the test. Bering took to his bed and supposed that he did it because there was nothing else he could do. And there was nothing else he could do if he intended to carry out this voyage with the strength that remained to him. But there were many other things which he might have done, or which another man might have done. He could have returned to Avacha, planning to make a voyage the following year. And he could have drunk the ship's brandy and forgotten visions. But Bering did none of these things.

The ship sailed north and then east and soon ran into thick weather. A green fog rolled about them or they sailed a steel-blue sea under a leaden sky. True sunshine was seldom seen. But the wind remained with them, and it was an easy, lazy voyage.

The ship's officers saw the empty sea and the empty sky and the long, empty days. But Steller's voyage was full of incidents. Soon after they set the course east he saw weeds tossing on the waves north of them. He inquired cautiously about the wind. It was from the southwest. That settled it. The drifting weed, not being carried by the wind, was carried by a current, which proved that land lay near them to the north. He went to the Commander's cabin and presented his evidence at great length. Bering showed very little interest.

"Surely you will turn north and investigate this land?" Steller asked in surprise.

"We have had many indications that land lies north of here," Bering explained. "But it also lies east—someplace. This course we are sailing was decided on in council, and I cannot abandon it to make other investigations."

"I am not speaking about indications! This evidence which I have brought you is as conclusive as if you had sighted land. And if that happened, you would certainly turn north." Seeing by the Commander's face that his argument had made no impression, Steller added angrily, "Or perhaps you want to run farther along the land, so that afterwards you can boast of having traveled very far and suffered very much—unnecessarily."

Bering ignored the insult. "This evidence is not conclusive. These weeds which you see may not have come from the land. In some parts of the ocean the whole sea is overgrown with them."

Steller had seen nothing strange in his telling the Commander how to direct the voyage, but that a sea captain should instruct him in botany was more than he could endure. He burst into a tirade.

"Do you think I am not aware of that fact? Do you think I can't tell you the places near Cape Verde and the Bermuda Islands where you find these seaweed drifting about? Do you want me to tell you their proper names? Do you want me to tell you how they are constructed and how they are transplanted? I can also tell you why such plants grow in those regions and not in the north!"

Steller saw Bering's face set as if a door had been closed.

"After you have decided on a course you do not change it for any reason?" he asked.

"No. I might change the course," Bering answered patiently. "But I would do it only on the advice of Master Khitrov."

Bering had said that he would change the course only on such advice as would come from Master Khitrov—soundings, the condition of the ship or the men, the amount of drinking water on board—but Steller understood him to say that the advice must come through Khitrov. He therefore took his arguments to Khitrov. He explained the weeds, the winds, and the current. For a few minutes Khitrov puzzled over what Steller was saying, and then his loud, hearty laugh rang through the ship. The sailors stopped their work and looked at him curiously.

Khitrov waved his arm to them and pointed at the sea. "The doctor can see a current out there!"

Soon every man on deck was laughing as one told another, "*He* can see a current in the sea!"

Steller never forgave this low-bred ridicule, but it did not keep him from his work. In a few days he caught some of the weed and examined it. It was a soft, smooth-stemmed grass which should have been torn and scattered after a short time at sea. He took this information to Khitrov. And again Khitrov laughed.

Steller saw the sea otter and pointed out the implications of this to the surgeon Betge. "The animal lives on crustaceans and shellfish and cannot, because of the structure of his heart, remain under water more than two minutes. He necessarily keeps close to shore because he cannot look for food at depths of sixty or a hundred fathoms—nor would he find any if he were able to." Betge looked interested but said nothing.

Steller saw flocks of gulls, always flying north—to the

mouths of rivers where fish would be plentiful—and pointed this out to Lieutenant Waxel. "How easy to follow them for just a few hours!" Waxel did nothing.

The officers, too, believed that land lay north of them, and when they had sailed too long without sighting anything they turned north. Actually this land was three hundred miles away; Steller believed that it was very near, only a few hours' sail. The officers could not judge his arguments, but there were other things which they did know. They were sailing in deep water with no bottom. They believed that they could not run close to shore for long without coming on a mountain peak or shoal water. And their course bore steadily north. They were passing naturally into the latitudes where Steller had before said there was land. That the land also bore north at about the same angle was something too improbable to consider.

On July seventeenth the course for the *St. Peter* was changed to north by east. Khitrov gives the reason for this in his journal. "If we were to continue on easterly courses we should be sailing farther and farther from Kamchatka, and not being able to replenish our supply of water, we should suffer great hardships and, may God preserve us, extreme misfortune. But in going northerly we stand a better chance of finding water for our needs."

But on that day the *St. Peter* had passed the easternmost of the Aleutian Islands and was opposite the tip of the Alaska Peninsula. At this point the coast too bears more sharply north, and by about the same amount. They continued to run parallel to the coast for another ten days.

On July twenty-seventh they sighted land—the high, snow-capped mountains of the St. Elias range on the American mainland. As they came closer they saw the heavily wooded slopes and a broad, sandy beach. Every man made as much noise as he could. They beat the drums, rang the bells, blew the trumpet, fired the cannons, and set off rockets. Everybody congratulated everybody else. Vodka was passed around on no one's order.

A European ship was standing off the west coast of America. A European captain looked at the pine forests and the range of snow-capped mountains. A trade route had been laid across the North Pacific and the last arm of the sea harnessed for man's use.

It was the first time Bering had left his cabin in three weeks. The despondency which had settled on him with the loss of the *St. Paul* had steadily deepened. His muscles throbbed with scurvy. Looking at the coast of America, he thought how much it resembled Siberia. This vision which had been his goal through fifteen long years had cost too much. The great accomplishment should have been the work of a young man who could feel glory, and who would live to profit from it. Bering was not thinking of Peter, or of the bedroom sixteen years before. He was thinking only of the lost Chirikov.

George Steller, sick with his own excitement, also looked at the land—a land no civilized eye had seen; a land that he would be the first to report on. The noise around him grated on his taut nerves. He felt a sudden, hot hatred for these men—men in shape only!—with whom he had nothing in common except that he was locked up in the same ship with them! Then he saw that the Commander had come on deck and was standing silent and unnoticed, looking toward the land.

Steller made his way to him and seized his hand. "We have reached the land! We are looking at a country which no civilized eye has ever seen! And it is to you the glory belongs. From now on you are immortal. Bering! A great name for all time!"

Bering looked at the land before him and shrugged his shoulders.

"Sir! Do you realize that we are in America?" asked the shocked Steller.

"Yes. We are in America. That is a long way from Kamchatka. And we shall probably have headwinds most of the way home."

The noise about him subsided. What Bering had said was so simple and so obvious that every member of the crew had understood it. They were in the prevailing westerlies. For six weeks they had run east with the wind. Now they must turn into it, make the same distance back against the wind. And they had ten or eleven weeks before the autumn gales.

9. ST. ELIAS DAY

STELLER had understood the seriousness of Bering's remark as fully as Khitrov. But his tense excitement had been jolted so rudely that he could only laugh. Every time he thought of the great moment when they looked at America, he laughed. "What did the great Commander say? What were his first words?" he asked, rehearsing a future conversation in Moscow. "The wind will probably be against us all the way back!"

In the meantime Khitrov had the responsibility of bringing the ship to rest. For two days he tacked north, following the shore, looking for an anchorage. It was an unfamiliar, mountainous coast and the local winds were unpredictable. During that time the west wind, which was the one to be expected, did not blow at all.

Steller, impatient to be ashore, found the delay unendurable. They were approaching an island when he again saw a current, this time plainly marked with floating debris. It came from a debouching glacier, but Steller knew nothing about glaciers. He told the master that east of the island was a large river mouth in which he could anchor.

"Have you been here before, or were you in God's cabinet?" Khitrov asked.

On July thirty-first, St. Elias Day, Khitrov dropped anchor in a cove on the west shore of an island and announced, "Cape St. Elias!" The drums and the bells sounded again and the crew cheered loudly for Cape St. Elias.

This island, which Khitrov meant to name St. Elias, still bears its Indian name, Kayak, due to the tense nerves on board the *St. Peter* that morning. "You can't name it that," Steller said, and, after allowing the men a minute to wonder what heresy was in St. Elias, added, "Because it's not a cape, it's an island." Khitrov immediately brought out his journal and wrote down "Cape St. Elias." So the record stood, and James Cook, who had Khitrov's record but not Steller's, was forced to enter in his journal, "I am unable to locate the promontory, Cape St. Elias." Unable to locate the cape, Cook gave the name to the mountain range.

Hearing the anchor go down, Bering came on deck and looked at their position. He assumed that this was the best anchorage to be found. But if the wind shifted to the west, the unwieldy brig would be landlocked.

"We must get out as quickly as we can," he said.

"We need water."

Bering nodded. "Send both boats. We must get away before night."

The longboat and the yawl were lowered and the empty water casks stowed in them. For a while Steller watched the activity, the shouting and the confusion, in silence, waiting his time. But slowly the realization came to him that he had been forgotten, that no preparations were being made for him.

"How am I to get ashore?" he asked Khitrov.

"Why should you get ashore?"

Steller turned to Bering in amazement, and saw by his unconcerned face that this meant nothing to him either! The unbelievable, terrible fact was true! He who had given years of his life, who had exiled himself from civilization and endured the snubs and insults of boorish officers in order to investigate a new world—he was to return without having touched a single leaf of it! Steller was frantic. In his excitement he forgot to speak Russian and lapsed into his native German.

"This is my work! This is my calling! My duty! You are forcing me to an inexcusable neglect of my duty. I shall report it to the Crown . . ."

Threatening and cursing, he became incoherent. The sailors, who thought he was mad, were frightened. But the officers, bored by weeks at sea, enjoyed the scene and goaded him.

"What a wild man to want to go ashore just when we're making chocolate!" Waxel said.

"Don't you know there are cannibals there?" Khitrov asked. "They would eat you!"

Steller suddenly controlled himself. He turned on Bering with an icy calm and asked, "Do you believe that the purpose of this expedition is to carry American water to Asia?"

"The expedition will serve no purpose at all if it does not return to Kamchatka," Bering answered. But Steller's desperate emotion had pained him, and he was shocked by the laughter of the officers. He asked angrily, "Why can't he go with the water boats, Master Khitrov? Make room for him and his man."

The boats pulled off toward the island. Steller had forgotten his anger and everything connected with the *St. Peter*. Before him lay the glory and the wonder of a new world. As the boat made its slow way to shore he gazed up at the mountains on the mainland beyond—not naked rocks covered with moss like the mountains of Siberia, but good black soil beautifully forested. Magnificent pines stood directly at the water's edge. In Kamchatka pines were only found forty miles inland, and in many places in Siberia there were no trees at all within three hundred miles of the sea.

As soon as the boat ground against the sand, Steller jumped out and started on a run for the forest. A flash of color stopped him. A bluejay had flown from one tree to another and now sat quietly on a branch before him. A song of joy rose in Steller's throat. There had been a colored plate of that very bird in a recent book on the Carolinas! Steller could not remember what the bird had been called. But its crested head and the blue and black markings on its wings and tail were unmistakable and sang to him that he was really in America.

His servant Thomas caught up with him while he was still looking at the bird and the two of them started into the forest together. Steller was carrying only a digging knife. Thomas had the gun.

"Don't fire that gun," Steller said, thinking of the uncertainties before them. "Don't even point it unless I tell you to."

A short distance into the forest, Steller came on a log which had been hollowed out in the shape of a trough. Meat had been roasted in it by means of hot stones. The stones were still warm and bones were scattered about on the ground where people had been sitting. Steller examined the bones. They were reindeer. He found pieces of dried fish such as the natives of Kamchatka used for bread, and there were half a dozen mussel shells sticky with a sweet liquid. The Kamchatkans made a syrup from grass, but this custom was peculiar to them and not known anyplace else in Siberia. Near the log Steller also found a Kamchatkan fire drill, but the dried moss which had been used for tinder was new to him.

The fish bread, the syrup, the fire drill were strange things

to find fifteen hundred miles from Kamchatka. Steller stood
for a few minutes turning over these facts in his mind. Then a
pile of freshly torn branches caught his eye. It was a clumsy,
childish attempt to hide a path which-led deeper into the forest,
and had probably been done while the ship lay in the bay. He
quickly pushed aside the brush and went down the path followed by Thomas.

After walking about a mile they came to a small clearing.
Here the ground was covered with cut grasses. Under the
grass Steller found bark laid over poles and under this a pit
about twelve feet deep. To climb down into this pit was to put
himself in a trap, but it was a storeroom, full of things he
wanted to examine, and after only a minute's hesitation Steller
went down.

He found bark jars filled with salmon, the cleanest, best-
prepared salmon he had ever seen. He tasted it, and it was far
superior to the salmon of Siberia. This was St. Elias Day, the
beginning of good fishing in Kamchatka, and here the winter
supply was already in. Steller, disposed to admire everything
he saw, marveled at the bountiful Nature which gave these
people such good fish so early. Near the jars was a pile of
thongs made from seaweed. Steller pulled on them to test their
strength. "They have very good rope." He found arrowheads,
larger than the ones used in Kamchatka, and carried them to
the light. They were as good as anything the Tartars had.
Examining them carefully, Steller was convinced that they had
been made with iron tools. Going back into the darkness of
the pit, he found a jar of liquid and tasted it. It was the
Kamchatka grass wine! It was better than the wine in Kamchatka—everything in this cellar was better—but it was unmistakable.

This wine was the secret of the Kamchatkans. No other
people in Siberia, not even their nearest neighbors, the Yakuts
and the Tungus, knew how to distill it. These people were

Kamchatkans! Steller gazed down the fifteen hundred miles they had traveled. As no native boat could travel such a distance, it was obvious that America stretched west to very near Kamchatka and that they had been skirting the coast through most of the voyage—as indeed he had thought all along.

He climbed out of the pit, taking some arrows and thongs and a sample of the fish with him. These things had told him so much that he supposed they would excite anyone, even Khitrov. He handed them to Thomas.

"Take these things to the Commander at once," he said. "Tell him I need two or three men to help me investigate further. Warn him that we may meet Americans at any minute. Hurry, Thomas."

Thomas was glad to leave the forest and hurried off, taking the gun with him. Steller, alone and unarmed, was afraid to go deeper into the woods and turned back toward the sea. But wherever he looked he saw something that excited him. He saw a raspberry bush—undoubtedly a raspberry—but the most beautiful, the most perfect bush he had ever seen, and with fruit an inch in diameter!

"That must be taken along with soil to St. Petersburg!" he said, and began to dig about the roots carefully. Looking up from his work, he saw a fox watching him from a short distance. Steller was more surprised than the fox.

"You aren't very much afraid of me, Mr. Reynard! The people here can't like your fur as much as we do!" The fox went on about its business in what Steller considered a very leisurely manner for a hunted animal.

The forest was full of birds. Steller saw the familiar magpie and raven, but otherwise they were all strange to him. They all differed from the birds of Europe and Siberia in their extremely high coloring

Climbing a steep hill, he was surprised to discover that the plants were the same size at the summit as they were at the base. That was never true in Siberia. At the top of the hill he found felled trees which had been miscut with the peculiar dull blow of the Kamchatkan bone axes. This seemed to argue that the people did not have iron.

Standing on the summit of the hill, Steller looked at the mainland, at the majestic range of snow-capped peaks. He supposed that his own work was the chief purpose of the expedition, and complained bitterly: "Ten years of laborious preparation, with great loss of life, and one short day ashore —not on the mainland itself, but on an island separated from it by a channel less than two miles wide! And why? Because a great expedition was entrusted to an ignorant man who can feel nothing but sluggish obstinacy and a cowardly homesickness!"

Steller's soliloquy stopped abruptly as he saw a gray wisp of smoke rising above the trees below him. Smoke! Men! He turned and ran down the hill and along the beach to the place where the sailors were loading water. This was no longer a theory, a peculiar deduction of a scientist. It was real. Anyone could understand it. He rushed up to the men breathless.

"Go at once to the Commander. Tell him Americans are here. I have seen their fire. I must have half a dozen men to interview them."

But the sailors refused to leave until they had filled their casks. Thomas had gone to the ship with the previous load of water and would not return till this one was delivered. There was nothing for Steller to do but wait. He moved away from the men, going a little distance up the stream, and suddenly found himself too tired to walk. He built a fire and made some tea. The tea revived him, and as the small plants he was carrying had already begun to wilt he spread them out on the pebbles and began to make sketches in his notebook. He was still busy with this when Thomas came along the stream toward him. Thomas was not bringing any other men!

"The Commander says that this is the last trip, and if you don't come on ship right away they will sail without you."

Steller, seized with a panic almost as great as that of the morning, dashed blindly into the forest. He went headlong, stumbling and tripping as he ran. Finally a fallen tree caught him across the body and he stopped. He heard the sighing of the pines and the small noises of birds and insects. The damp, loamy smell of the earth rose around him. He lifted his arms toward the vault of the forest and groaned. It was too much, too great. How could he take any of it with him? He walked slowly back to the place where he had left Thomas, for once in his life seeing nothing.

At the fire he saw the raspberry bush and picked it up tenderly. But no. Space would be begrudged. He himself took up too much space as it was. Dropping the bush, he went on toward the sea with Thomas. But Steller was still in a new world and his gloom could not last. Coming out of the woods, he saw a number of small brown piles on the sand.

"What is that?" he asked excitedly.

Thomas looked. "It's dung."

"I know that!" Steller said, stooping down to examine it. When he stood up his face was shining.

"Otter dung! Thomas, the sea otter comes ashore here!"

Thomas shrugged his shoulders. But on the coasts of Siberia, where the sea otter did not come ashore, it was hunted over drift ice at enormous risk.

"The sea otter breeds in America!" Steller said, his voice trembling with awe.

When Steller came on board ship, to his great astonishment the officers invited him to have chocolate with them. They looked at the things he had brought and asked questions about them, trying to make amends for the morning. But Steller could not respond to this friendliness. He had exchanged the noises of the pine forest for the roll and creak of the ship, the excitement of discovery for the conversation of stupid officers.

Bering came into the cabin to listen to what Steller had to say. "I have sent ashore some Chinese silk and tobacco to pay the Americans for what you took," he told him.

"If we ever come to these parts again we must expect the natives to be hostile," Steller said sullenly. "They can hardly know the use of tobacco, and if they attempt to eat it or drink it they will assume that we meant to poison them. Knives or hatchets, the use of which is quite obvious, would have been a more suitable gift."

Two knives, an iron kettle, and a pipe had been sent ashore with the silk and tobacco. But no one told Steller this. Waxel said:

"Knives might be regarded as a sign of hostility. The Americans might take such a present to be a declaration of war."

The ship was moving out of the bay, and Steller went on deck. As long as light lasted he stood at the rail looking at the beautiful country they were leaving. Such a superior country, so unlike Siberia in every way! He had been particularly pleased with the orderly manner in which water issued from the ground. "In America streams flow out of the valleys at the base of the mountains and not, as in Siberia, anywhere among the rocks, even on the very summits." Such rich vegetation must be well sheltered from the winds. "I believe the land runs north from here as far as 70," he said. He already believed that it ran west as far as Kamchatka. Such firm, well-shaped mountains would certainly contain precious minerals. Why were they leaving this country? Because the wind blew favorably for getting out of harbor and contrary for going in—and to the mind of the Commander that was reason enough.

He turned around and saw the detested Khitrov overseeing the men at their work of taking the ship out of harbor. Then, lifting his voice so that the sailors could hear him, Steller cursed the expedition.

"We can hardly expect God's help on the return voyage!" he shouted. "But wind and water will treat us as we have treated our duty, and our good fortune!"

1O. THE VOYAGE OF THE "ST. PAUL"

FOR THREE DAYS the *St. Paul* was blown off her course to the south. On the third day Chirikov, feeling that the time he should have spent looking for the *St. Peter* had already passed, set the course east for America without making any attempt to return north.

The weeks passed quickly in the cabin of the *St. Paul*. There was no grim Commander, no anxious Steller to mar the voyage. Chirikov, a captain who had never been to sea, lived with his officers. The time was filled with cards and songs and the curious stories of Louis Delisle. In the drawing room and among the scientists Louis Delisle had been the bored man who found nothing worth his interest, but here in an empty world, where other men were bored, nothing was too small to rouse his interest. A shift of the wind, a turn of the cards, would bring amazing stories out of his vagabond life. The young officers listened agape at the sophistication which stepped so lightly from the strange people of Baffin's Bay to the strange people of Paris. Removed from the opinions of the Academists, and seeing Louis against the young officers, Chirikov admired him immensely and laughed uproariously at his stories.

The shipmaster Dementiev and the navigator Elagin belonged by rank in the cabin with the naval officers—in fact the cabin belonged to them and the naval officers were their guests. But Dementiev found the company too brilliant, the discrepancy between himself and the lieutenants too great, and moved into the quarters of the petty officers.

"I'm master of this ship," he said, "and I have the right to be comfortable."

Elagin was compelled to go with his superior. He would have enjoyed the singing and the laughter, and he believed the friendship of these officers would have been profitable to him later. As it was, he did most of their work for them. They thanked him warmly and praised the work more than it deserved. But they did not think of giving him their companionship, simply because he did not bunk with them, and Elagin found the outward voyage a bitter one.

On July twenty-fifth they saw large numbers of shore duck and knew that land was near. At dawn on the twenty-sixth it was silhouetted against the brightening sky. The *St. Paul* had reached land at the Alexander Archipelago, several hundred miles south of Kayak Island. It was an irregular, mountainous coast, heavily timbered. The crew cheered the success of the voyage and each man was given an extra cup of brandy. The *St. Paul* moved in toward shore but without finding water shallow enough for the anchor.

That night brought fog, and the ship put back to sea. Following the plan agreed on at the council, they turned north, skirting the coast which loomed through the mist. They sailed for two days, sounding constantly without finding bottom. On July twenty-eighth the fog cleared and they saw the coast. It was covered with deep snow. To the north rose Mount Fairweather in the St. Elias range.

This was glacier country, and snow did not lie on the coasts farther north. It was fjord water, full of unpredictable currents and rips. But Chirikov and his men were frightened by the unexpected winter and afraid to go further without taking on water. They believed they would be sailing into colder country and that the longer they waited, the more difficult the landing would be. It was decided to send Dementiev and ten soldiers ashore with the longboat to get water.

Everyone was aware that this was a great moment, that they were making a first landing on an unknown coast and thereby taking possession of the country for Russia. Dementiev was schooled in what he was to do, and examined by Chirikov in the presence of the officers.

"If I cannot make a landing I am to return immediately to the ship. If bad weather sets in while I am ashore, so that I cannot return to the ship, I am to light a fire on the beach and keep it night and day."

"What presents are you taking with you for the inhabitants?"

"I have a copper kettle, an iron one, two hundred beads, three pieces of tobacco, a piece of cloth, and a paper of needles."

Now that the hour had come, these gifts seemed small to Chirikov. He drew out his purse. "Let me add ten rubles. Distribute them among the Americans as you think best. You understand that you are to be gentle with these people. If they behave toward you in an unfriendly manner return to the ship as quickly as possible. But do not harm them. Ask some of them to come with you. The Admiralty is anxious to have us bring a few of these people back with us. Do you know what questions you are going to ask?"

"I am going to ask them what kind of land this is, what government they are under, and what rivers flow into the sea."

Chirikov was searching among the papers before him. "Naturally you will observe what kinds of trees there are. Ah! Here it is!" He picked up a small piece of metal and handed it to Dementiev. "Do you know what this is?"

"No sir. It might be something from a harness."

"Never mind that. It is a piece of natural silver. We are very anxious to know something about the minerals of this country. So while you are ashore keep your eyes open, and if you see anything that looks like this, bring it back to the ship."

The longboat put off and an hour later had disappeared into the bay. As it was impossible to anchor in the deep water, the *St. Paul* tacked along the coast. When night came she moved further out to sea for safety. The next morning brought wind and heavy rain, which was followed by three days of fog. St. Elias Day passed unnoticed. Several times the *St. Paul* came close to shore, but all landmarks were blurred and she could not be certain of her position. However, those on land had enough food with them to last a week.

On the fifth day following the lowering of the boat the fog lifted and the *St. Paul* returned to the bay. They believed they saw a column of smoke on the beach, and after night the fire showed plainly. A gun was fired from the *St. Paul*. There was no answering sound from the shore, though the longboat carried cannon. But the fire seemed to leap higher. Seven times the gun was fired as a signal for the men to come on board, and each time it seemed as if the fire blazed up.

Chirikov called his officers in council. It seemed probable that the longboat had been damaged in landing and that the men were stranded. In that case the carpenter and calker should be sent ashore to repair the boat. But the *St. Paul* now had only the yawl; it was impossible to send soldiers with the men, and if the fire on shore was not Dementiev's, but that of some enemy people, these men would be entirely at their mercy. The officers were thinking only of the four men who would go in the small boat and the risks they might be exposed to. What might happen to the ship if they lost both boats and the carpenter, it did not occur to them to wonder.

After very little deliberation it was decided that they could not sail without attempting to rescue their men. The carpenter and calker were willing enough to go, and two sailors volunteered to take them. These men were given no instructions about investigating the country. They were simply told to fire a rocket immediately on landing and to send back Dementiev and as many men as the small boat would carry, at once.

The sea was unusually still. There was a light wind and the *St. Paul* was able to follow the little boat at a distance. They watched it approaching shore, the *St. Paul* close enough to make out rocks awash and the surf breaking on them. But no rocket was fired. The *St. Paul* hove to and waited. The wind had fallen and the ship made almost no headway. Those on shore had the weather in their favor for coming out. But no boat appeared. The *St. Paul* fired her guns but got no response. When night fell a lantern was hung on the ensign staff, but with the night the *St. Paul* was obliged to move out to sea.

The next morning they returned to the bay and again sailed as close to shore as wind and rocks would permit. After waiting several hours they were relieved to see two small boats coming toward them. The crew had assembled on deck and were getting the hoisting ropes ready, when suddenly a shout went up from the *St. Paul*. The boats had come close enough for it to be seen that the men in them were not rowing. They were paddling, like the natives of Kamchatka! A few minutes later a figure in red stood up and shouted, "*Agai! Agai!*" Then both boats turned about and made for the shore.

Chirikov called to his men to wave white handkerchiefs and invite the Americans aboard. Some handkerchiefs appeared but had no effect on the Americans. The boats continued to pull away and finally disappeared into the bay from which

they had come. The *St. Paul* could not follow. Between her
and the shore were rocks. And there was no wind.

Everyone felt that the Americans had behaved in a very
suspicious manner. Why should they have been afraid to approach the ship, unless they had already done some harm to
the men ashore? That night the fire was again seen on the
beach. But no further landing was possible. Whether Dementiev and his men were dead or merely facing death from starvation, they were equally beyond help from the *St. Paul*. The
next day there was still a column of smoke, but the ship put
out to sea.

So ended the geographic and mineralogical investigations of
the *St. Paul*. What became of the men is not known. Eighty
years later, in 1820, the Russian governor at Sitka received a
sharp reprimand from his government for not having found
them in such a long time. Wages were due them, and someone
in St. Petersburg wanted to pay the money and close the
books. But no trace of them was ever found. What happened
can only be conjectured. Chirikov believed that his men came
to grief at the hands of the Americans. But it is more likely
that their enemy was a current which capsized the boats.

The loss of the fifteen men disturbed Chirikov greatly. But
that was the small part of the calamity. There were now sixty
men aboard ship, with no way of getting drinking water but
to return to Avacha for it. The chief item in these men's food
was a buckwheat mush which could not be cooked without
water. The ship was immediately put on one cooked meal a
day, and this was soon changed to one meal every other day.
Buckets were set under the dripping sails and this water used
to supplement the drinking ration. It tasted strongly of tar,
but the men said its bitter flavor would keep off scurvy. The
crew accepted their privations with good humor, but the cold,
wet fogs they were sailing in made hot foods a necessity.

The *St. Paul* had reached America six weeks after leaving Avacha, but eleven weeks were spent making the return voyage. This was partly due to headwinds and partly to the land. They were attempting to make the westward voyage three hundred miles north of the course they had sailed going east. On the outward voyage there had been no signs of land. Now they could not get away from it. The coast, which they knew was at hand, remained hidden in the mists, but they saw signs of it continually—ducks, driftwood, and shallow water. Land now meant nothing to them but the danger of running aground, and again and again they moved south to avoid it.

On September nineteenth the *St. Paul* had covered a little less than half the distance home and was close to the island Adak. That day they had many signs of land—floating grasses and a shallow bottom. Toward evening they heard the sound of breaking surf. Afraid to go on, they dropped anchor and waited. At noon the next day the fog thinned and showed land less than a quarter of a mile from the ship. A little later the air had cleared completely and they saw the high hills and a snow-covered volcano in the distance.

The coast they were facing was bare of trees but covered with tall grasses. On a cliff near the sea two men were walking through the grass. Then the crew of the *St. Paul* saw a brook running down the hill at about the place where the men were standing. Clear, cold water! They began to shout and the men on shore answered. The syllables were drowned in the noise of the breakers, but the men on ship heard distinctly the thin small sound of the human voice.

An hour later seven boats put off from shore. Each boat held one man. When these men were about a hundred yards from the ship they began to shout, swaying their bodies from side to side. The Russians could hear that this was ceremonial talking, an incantation of some kind. After a few minutes it stopped and the men called to one another in normal tones.

Chirikov had concealed his soldiers and, most of the crew. Only a few men stood on deck watching the Americans. Chirikov commanded them to look pleasant. They did this by placing their hands over their hearts and bowing. The Americans in turn were making the gesture of drawing a bow.

So matters stood for some time while the interpreter asked questions in all the languages he knew. Chirikov observed that the strangers were surprisingly light skinned and that they resembled the Tartars of Siberia—that is, they were Mongolian. Finally, seeing that the interpreter knew nothing about their language, he took matters into his own hands and threw one of them a Chinese cup. The man examined it and would have thrown it back to the ship, but Chirikov motioned to him to keep it. Whereupon the man dropped it in the sea. Other gifts followed—damask, bells, needles, and tobacco. Each thing was examined and then cast aside. The needles, however, aroused interest. The Americans were surprised that they sank and watched them go down with pleasure.

Chirikov wanted his gifts to show good will. He was anxious to get the Americans on board to show them how friendly he was. The strangers understood his beckoning but could not be coaxed onto the ship. In fact they would not even come close enough to be caught and dragged onto the ship. Chirikov, with fifty armed men lying under cover, was surprised and puzzled by this timidity.

During all this time the Americans had been putting both hands to their mouths in a quick, sharp gesture. Suddenly Chirikov saw that they were cutting off bites of meat. He ordered a knife given to them. At sight of the knife the Americans became very excited. They seized it from one another, shouting among themselves.

Here, almost a thousand miles from the coast of Siberia, were men who knew knives. These islanders had got their few knives from men like themselves, who in turn had got them from other men like themselves—all equally incapable of making the miraculous tool, or even of imagining how it could be made. When that great, goose-winged ship appeared on their coast, as likely to have strayed from the skies as from anything they knew on earth, this miracle was immediately comparable to the miracle of knives. The islanders had gone out to meet the strange and the terrifying in the hope that it might be the source of knives. And a knife had appeared! They clamored for more.

Having discovered the effectiveness of sign language, Chirikov showed the Americans that he and his men wanted drinking water from the stream on shore. He was understood at once. Moreover, the Americans, surprised by this human need, lost a good deal of their fear and came closer to the ship. Chirikov showed them a cask which he wanted filled. They understood what he wanted but showed him that *they* carried water in bladders and in their present situation had no mind to do anything in the least irregular. Chirikov indicated that they should get water in whatever container was proper, and three men paddled to the shore. When they returned one of them held up the bladder and demanded a knife. When this was given to him he passed the bladder to the second man, who also demanded a knife and then passed it to the third. For three knives the *St. Paul* received one bladder of drinking water.

The islanders had no way of knowing that there were more than a dozen men on the ship, and they could not imagine that these men would not return to their home that day or the next. But Chirikov, weak with long starvation and exhausted by scurvy, could not see this with the eyes of the Americans. He had sixty men nearing death from lack of water; the water was in sight on shore. And between them were human beings who could bring it and would not. He wrote in his journal, "This, as well as some other things they did, proves that their conscience is not highly developed." Perhaps the other things were dropping good manufactured articles into the sea.

About six o'clock in the evening a light breeze lifted the sails. A storm was gathering on the other side of the mountain. They began to heave the anchor, but before they could get it in a squall struck the ship and they were driven toward shore. They cut the cable and crowded on all sails, and an hour later had cleared the land. But they had had a narrow escape from danger.

Twice the *St. Paul* had touched the American coast and seen the American people. And each time they had found the people as inhospitable as their shores.

The *St. Paul* was at sea five weeks after the encounter with the American "fleet." The water supply was so low at that time that the ship was put on one cooked meal a week. This was in effect for one week, after which there were no cooked meals at all. The seven men who died under these conditions were said to have died of scurvy. For some reason the officers were more affected than the crew. This can hardly have been due to the flavor of tar in the men's drinking water. But, for whatever reason, after the eighth week none of the officers was able to leave his bed, and by the time the *St. Paul* reached Avacha all but Chirikov and Louis Delisle were dead.

Elagin now had charge of the ship and slept in the cabin. The young officers, only half conscious, moaned in their bunks. Louis Delisle lay with his eyes open, staring at the planks above him, watching the slow movement of death as he had watched other phases of life. But he did not laugh. As the only officer able to be on deck, Elagin was on deck continually and went below only for a few hours at a time, and then delirious with exhaustion.

On October twentieth he entered Chirikov's cabin quietly,

expecting the captain to be asleep. But he was sitting against the pillows, an inkpot near him and papers on his knees.

"Captain, we are in Avacha Bay."

Chirikov, too weak to feel elation, received the news indifferently. "Drop the anchor and signal with the guns. We will be towed into harbor."

He turned back to his work mechanically, almost unconsciously, performing a duty. Whether or not he lived, he must send a report to the Admiralty College.

"Of the company that was put under my command, some by the will of God died at sea and others were lost on the American coast. I have left only one man on board for managing the ship, and that is the navigator Elagin. If it had not been for him and the strength which God gave him, some great misfortune would have happened to the ship.

"As to myself, I am quite unfit for sea duty. By God's mercy I am able to sit up, but my feet are drawn up and full of spots and the teeth are loose in my gums. A similar state of ill-health exists among the crew, most of whom are not fit for service."

Elagin came into the cabin again. "The anchor is down, sir —and Professor Delisle is dead."

The pen slipped from Chirikov's fingers and he sank on the pillows. They had all gone—the young lieutenants with their curiosity and their hopes, and the man who had been his friend through ten bleak years. He remembered the evening at Joseph Delisle's—the hopes, the excitement, and the ambitious plans. They were to do so much! And he had done nothing. He heard the excited voices arguing about native peoples. He had been instructed to look into those things. He sat up again. He must not appear to have ignored his instructions. It must be stated clearly that he had been unable to carry them out. He took up his papers and wrote again.

"According to the instructions of the Admiralty College

we were required to bring to St. Petersburg a few inhabitants of the newly discovered land, or of land we might discover in the future. We could not persuade them to come. Not having any of these people with mé and not knowing their language, I can say little about them."

He took up the instructions, which had once been so glorious, and turned through them to see what else he had failed to do. Then he added a final paragraph.

"The instructions of the Admiralty College require that this report be sent in care of an officer who took part in the expedition. Unfortunately that is not possible, as all the officers are dead."

11. SCURVY

CHIRIKOV supposed that the loss of his two boats brought the *St. Paul* to grief. But actually the loss of the boats brought her to port. Time meant more than food or water, and because the *St. Paul* had no water and no boats, she went direct to Avacha. On the day the *St. Paul* lost her seventh man the *St. Peter* had lost two. But on that day the *St. Paul* had reached port, while the *St. Peter* was being driven off her course by the autumn storms.

In making the homeward voyage the *St. Peter* started further north and sailed closer to the land than the *St. Paul* had done. She frequently ran into such shallow water that it was necessary to drop anchor and wait for clearer air before going on.

Shallow water, ducks, new-fallen trees, were things the officers could understand, and the chart they made of the

American coast is amazingly accurate. At first the land occasionally seen through the mists was heavily wooded—arguing a sheltered coast, a mainland stretching far to the north. But after the first month they began to see stunted trees, and finally no trees at all. Sighting land only at intervals, Bering's men never knew that it was a chain of islands they were skirting. But they did know that it was wind-swept, that it had narrowed suddenly, and believed that America stretched toward Kamchatka in a long, very narrow peninsula.

They sailed continually in fog, a gray circle of sea that did not change. Sometimes the green smoke streaked in wisps from the mast. Sometimes the heavy sky came down in snow; sometimes it lifted on a calm gray world. But it never actually cleared.

During the fifth week of the homeward voyage the *St. Peter* and *St. Paul* were within fifty miles of one another. They had made about a quarter of the distance home, and the drinking water was again low on board the *St. Peter*. She therefore turned north to make a landing and on September ninth dropped anchor among some small islands, beyond which could be seen the mainland.

Water casks were again stowed in the boats and taken ashore. But while they were being filled the boats returned to the ship. There were a number of men on board sick with scurvy, and half a dozen of these were taken ashore to rest. One, a sailor, Nikita Shumagin, died as soon as he was put down on land.

This first death from scurvy was the signal that they had been at sea too long. Steller asked for a detail of men to gather herbs and was refused, doubtless because the officers did not understand that it was medicine he was thinking of, and supposed it was pure science. Steller, who had expected this answer, considered that he had fulfilled his duty to the ship and gathered leaves and anti-scurvy berries (cranberries) for

himself. In the meantime the sailors had found a fresh-
water lake and were filling the casks. Steller examined the
water and sent a report to the ship saying it was brackish and
recommending another watering place. But this recommenda-
tion was disregarded.

Toward evening a strong wind began to blow. It was necessary to send the longboat for Khitrov, who could not get
off shore in the yawl. The sick were hurriedly brought on
ship and Nikita Shumagin buried, giving the islands his name
with his body. Before morning the wind had risen to a gale.

The storm continued for a week. The wind was toward the
west, but the St. Peter was held there, locked among the
islands by winds and heavy fog. During that week the same
wind carried the St. Paul five hundred miles toward home.

On the fifth day of the storm, as the ship lay at anchor in
the shelter of an island, two small boats put out from shore
and paddled toward them. The St. Peter's men did not attempt to look pleasant. They merely beckoned with their
hands for the Americans to come closer.

The Americans, having observed the ship standing offshore
for five days, made gestures of eating and drinking and
pointed to the land, inviting the strangers to come and eat
with them. The interpreters spoke to them in Koriak and
Chukchi, and the Americans showed that they did not understand by pointing to their ears. In the meantime more men
had appeared on the beach, and these kept up a constant
shouting to their companions in the boats. Steller puzzled over
this and was unable to see the purpose of it. The Americans
made the first gift—a pair of falcon wings tied to a spruce
wand—and in return were given a pipe and some glass beads,
which they laid carefully on their boats. After a little while
they pulled away for shore, beckoning the strangers to follow.

Bering ordered the longboat lowered, and Waxel, taking

twelve men with him, went as close to shore as he dared. The strong wind and heavy surf made it impossible to land, but several men, among them the Koriak interpreter, undressed and waded ashore. Steller remained in the boat but saw everything that happened on the beach. He saw that the Americans singled out the Koriak, who resembled them a great deal, and treated him as the principal personage. They led him to a place near the fire and presented him with blubber which he drank gladly. Steller noticed that the Americans constantly pointed to the mainland and were talking about the mainland. These people called the mainland Alaska. Steller supposed they were saying that they lived there and not on these islands. But as that was not the case, they were probably asking whether the strangers came from Alaska.

While this was going on at the fire the less-important Americans stood near the water looking at the longboat and talking about the men in it. Finally one got into his canoe and came out to them. Waxel, having nothing else to give, offered him a drink of brandy. Steller cried out in alarm, but Waxel insisted.

"These Americans are sailors, and they have sailors' stomachs," he said.

What the man's stomach was like, they did not learn. As the brandy burned his throat he spit it out in surprise and paddled away from them, annoyed by the practical joke.

After half an hour, as the wind was blowing stronger, Waxel called the men back to the boat. But the Americans had only begun their festivities and caught hold of their guests to keep them by force. Others ran into the water and caught hold of the boat to draw it on shore. The Russians lifted their muskets, but as the Americans had never seen guns the threat meant nothing. The longboat was in danger of being crushed against the rocks by the hospitable islanders, and Waxel ordered his men to fire in the air. With the sudden noise the

Americans fell, on their faces and the Russians got away. The Americans were soon on their feet again, scolding the guests who had behaved so uncivilly, and waving to them to be gone.

Bering had found land further north than Chirikov, and found it fertile; he had met the savages further from civilization, and found them gracious. Two days later the *St. Peter* moved out to sea. They had taken on water, which according to Steller was alkaline, and they had made some observations of the American people. But these things had cost them their return to Avacha.

The islands sank into the horizon, and in a few hours the ship had returned to the sea—to the cold, the wet, and the racking strain of dangers which could not be seen, to the rolling fog that dripped from the sails and the cries of men who fought in the fog for breath.

The courage of the men dropped suddenly. For a little longer Betge, the German surgeon, made out the sick list and passed on who was able to work and who wasn't. But this was soon out of Betge's hands. In a few weeks no one was able to work. Then there was no question of obedience or disobedience. The safety of the ship depended solely on a blind sense of responsibility, working automatically and unreasonably in half-conscious men.

When a man has scurvy he is eating foods that give energy but not what is needed to repair tissue, and if he works he destroys his own flesh. The disease begins with weariness, discouragement, and a disinclination to work. As it deepens, to move a muscle becomes painful, and no work worth doing. Finally some organ—the lungs, the kidneys, the intestines— gives way and the man dies. The despair that accompanies scurvy is more blinding than the fog. Reason has no power against the driving need for quiet, and what a man will do rests simply on what he is.

Aboard the *St. Peter*, when a man reached the point of exhaustion where he no longer cared what became of himself or the ship, he was sick. He then lay on the deck without knowing what went on around him. After a time, a few hours or a few days, something would speak to him. Perhaps it would be a yard that had swung free and had to be caught. It had to be lashed. Knowing only that, the sick man would get to his feet. Before he had it fastened securely, his mind would clear. He would see four men at the mainmast, struggling with the huge canvas; he would see all that had to be done if the ship was to come to port. He became one of the "able-bodied" until hopelessness overwhelmed him again.

There were men aboard the *St. Peter* who could not be wakened by the gravest danger and there were others, like Waxel and Khitrov, who never gave up. All were ravaged with scurvy, but anyone who was conscious at all knew that without desperate heroism on everyone's part, they would all die at sea. The combined will power of that crew kept ten men on their feet after no one was able to stand—not for a few days, but for ten weeks. As long as Khitrov called them, the stunned, half-conscious men responded with that minimum.

Steller knew a great deal about scurvy before he sailed on the *St. Peter*. But this desperate courage was something he could not understand. Again and again he saw the dying get to their feet and go to work, and he lost faith in the reality of the disease. He already believed that Bering was suffering from "too much inactivity" and decided that the men's sickness was due to "cold, dampness, nakedness, vermin, and fright."

A few days after they had left the islands and returned to the sea, the singing and the shouting had ceased. The men stood in small groups and talked quietly.

"I say another week and we'll have the gales," said a cannoneer. "And how far have we come in eight weeks?"

The men looked at Ovtsin. They looked to him for everything. He was a great man, who had ranked higher than Waxel or Khitrov. And he was one of them; he would tell them the truth.

"We have come less than halfway in eight weeks," Ovtsin said.

Khitrov watched the men and waited. He knew that they were restless. He knew that Ovtsin was keeping them stirred up. "A degraded officer always makes trouble," he told himself. "I'd rather see a sailor in command than an officer in the ranks."

Steller spent a great deal of time on deck. A thick fog drove him below to the cabin, where he had to endure the company of the officers and listen to their trivial, irritating talk. But the thin fog did not touch him and he did not see it at all. He placed his materials securely inside a coil of rope and worked at his sketches undisturbed.

The sailors kept away from him. His strange aloofness to the ship and everything in it gave him an uncanny quality, and in addition to their solid fears about the winds, the men had a superstitious fear of him.

"Is he flesh?" they asked.

"He's flesh. But the devil has him under his wing."

Steller was unaware of the change in the ship for some time, but at last the unnatural silence, the lack of singing, made itself felt. A strange chill came over him and he put down his work. Everything was deathly still! Something must be wrong, and someone must be to blame.

He remembered that the Commander's cabin was just below him. There, under his feet, that old man slept, week after week! That was doubtless the cause of everyone's uneasiness. Steller half rose to his feet. "I shall tell him! At his age such indolence is dangerous."

At that moment there was a stir on deck. A man was reefing

a sail and the rotten hemp broke in his hands. He dropped to the deck and laughed while the canvas bellied in the wind. Khitrov went toward him but he made no move to go back to his work. He said something and Khitrov knocked him down. Then Steller saw the faces of the other men. No one was working. They were all watching Khitrov. The master bore down, first on one, then on another; four times he gave the order "Get on with it!" where one shout should have done.

Steller turned and looked at the sick lying on the deck near him. These were men who could not be moved; they lay where they had fallen and screamed if they were touched. But now, here and there among them, one turned his head and looked at Khitrov with the same menacing expression that was in the eyes of the able-bodied. It was this slight stir among the dying that sent the terror into Steller's heart. Then he remembered the officers sitting in the cabin and his horror changed to fury. So that was why he could never get the table to himself! They were afraid to come on deck! With trembling hands he stuffed his papers into a leather bag and went below.

The officers were all there. Waxel sat with his feet on the table, smoking a pipe. Steller laid his bag with his blankets and went up to the lieutenant.

"What is the matter with the men?" he demanded.

Waxel answered indifferently, "They're frightened. The time for gales is close and we're a thousand miles from Avacha."

His matter-of-fact tone infuriated Steller. "The men are afraid of the weather," he said. "And you are afraid of the men! Isn't that true?"

"Yes, that is true. And the men are quite right. We cannot possibly reach Avacha, but we keep on going."

Waxel brought his feet to the floor and reached for the sick list. It was not the men he was afraid to face. He believed that

he had a duty to them, to get them ashore. But he also had a
duty to the Admiralty, to carry out orders. He believed that,
left to himself, he could have solved this conflict and landed
the men without defying the Commander. But he was not left
to himself. Every time he stepped on deck he saw Ovtsin's
eyes fixed on him, eyes that understood and condemned.
Ovtsin's eyes did more than condemn; they said, "You are
about to commit an act of insubordination. I will report it to
St. Petersburg." Waxel put down the sick list without looking
at it. Men like Ovtsin didn't get sick.

Steller sat down at the table. The men who had been standing near unconsciously moved away. At the beginning of the
voyage a natural dislike for this man had made him the butt
of their jokes. But dislike had deepened to aversion, and Steller now repelled them physically. They were not particularly
aware of this because they did not talk about him or think
about him; they simply moved away.

Betge, the surgeon, had come in from the Commander's
cabin and was pouring himself a glass of brandy. Betge was a
good surgeon. He could amputate a leg or explore an abdomen regardless of the havoc around his operating table.
Most of the men he operated on died, but he knew, and everybody knew, that all that could have been done for them had
been done. And they died quickly. Watching the long, slow
death from scurvy exhausted him horribly. Sometimes he
physicked his patient, sometimes he bled him; but he had no
faith in anything he did. Sometimes for a whole week he did
nothing at all. Bering lay in his bed with half-closed eyes; he
seldom spoke. Because there was nothing else he could do,
Betge felt that he owed his Commander his company. He
would sit in the cabin, facing the sick man, thinking of nothing at all, until the strain became unbearable. Then he would
join the officers for an hour's relaxation. He would pour himself a brandy and tell them about operations he had performed

or witnessed or heard about. The officers, who understood conversation as a release, understood Betge and found no fault with his stories.

This time, after swallowing his brandy, Betge said, "Scurvy is the worst thing there is, because there is nothing you can do about it!" He had succeeded in putting into words the tension of the room beyond.

Steller seldom joined these discussions, but this was a subject which interested him. "On the contrary, Doctor," he said emphatically, "scurvy is very easy to handle. A little cedar tea will clear it up in a few days."

Steller saw Betge's pale blue eyes staring uncomprehendingly and thought, "It is amazing how many men do not know the simplest facts about their own trade!" He went on aloud, "Perhaps you do not know, but I was once physician to the Bishop of Novgorod. I know something about medicine."

Steller misunderstood the bewilderment in Betge's face. The surgeon knew very well that cedar water relieved scurvy. He was wondering if the *St. Peter* was really at sea. "Cedar tea?" he asked himself. "He says, 'Give him cedar tea.' Where do I get the cedar?"

Steller was saying, "The Commander's illness is largely due to indolence anyway. If he would get up and do something he wouldn't be sick."

Betge sat down at the table relieved. He knew now which of them was mad. Steller went on, "As for the men"—indolence could hardly be attributed to them—"I think the chief cause of their trouble is the unwholesome water taken aboard."

Steller's constant harping on the water annoyed everyone. Betge said sullenly, "Any man who's been at sea four months has scurvy."

"I haven't. Not a touch of it."

The casually spoken words startled everyone; all eyes were fixed on Steller as each man slowly realized the significance of this fact. It was quite true. He moved his arms and legs without effort; there was nothing strained in his face. And that was what was horrible about him! That was what repelled them. In the general sickness of the ship, health itself was ghoulish.

Steller was pleased to have made an impression on these men. "While you were loading the ship with tainted water," he explained, "I busied myself with gathering cress and docks. And you see the results."

The men were still staring at him. Waxel leaned across the table and spoke slowly, weighting each word. "You found medicinal plants on the island, and you took just enough for yourself?" he asked.

"That is just what I did," said Steller. "I asked the ship-master for a detail of men to help me gather herbs, but my work was not considered worth the labor of a few sailors and I was refused. So I resolved to look after my own preservation and waste no more words."

One by one the men left the room, not as an intentional insult, but simply to get away. Waxel too went on deck. He saw Khitrov standing by the rail and went over to him. They stood in silence watching the silent ship.

Waxel had forgotten about Steller. His mind had returned to the serious problem: could insubordination ever be a soldier's duty?

"He is dying," he said at last, lowering his voice at the awful word. "He does not know what he is doing. Under his will we are all sailing to our deaths."

Khitrov nodded, and Waxel felt a great relief. If the master was with him, the problem was half solved. But what remained would not be easy.

"His will is a strong wind to turn against," he said.

12. HEADWINDS

ON OCTOBER SIXTH the *St. Peter* was caught in a typhoon and for three weeks was carried to the eastward. During the afternoon of the fifth they had unusually clear weather and sighted Adak, the island where Chirikov had bargained for water three weeks before. They saw the snow-capped volcano in the distance and supposed it was on the American mainland. During the night they had rain and a heavy swell and before morning a gale was blowing.

Then the storm came. The noise of the wind was deafening. It screamed and whistled in the rigging. The sea pounded the hull and rain swept over the deck in solid sheets. Sometimes this changed to hail. Sometimes the sea washed over them from both sides at once. Sails were torn, ropes snapped, and the hull shuddered and creaked as if about to split apart.

On the sixth day of the storm the wind went down but the sea was still running heavily. They believed that the storm had passed, but they were crossing the center and that night it struck again with even greater violence. No one could hold the wheel, and the ship tossed on the waves like driftwood. The sick shrieked as they rolled about in the darkness.

George Steller pulled himself to the deserted deck and looked around. Half the ship was under water. Waves and spray rose in a gray wall about them and he could not see six feet beyond the rail. Overhead the clouds shot past like arrows. They met and crossed each other, coming from opposite directions at the same incredible speed.

On the tenth day of the storm a stay on the starboard side of the mainmast gave way and the great pole was at the mercy of the wind. Waxel stumbled into the cabin, clutching the door for support. He saw the mate Esselberg pulling himself along by the wall. Waxel's eyes, fixed on the mate's flowing white hair, asked, "You have seen such things before?"

Esselberg shook his head. "In fifty years at sea I never saw anything like it!" he whispered.

The ship lurched violently and made a sudden stop. Both men were thrown against the wall and then to the rear of the cabin as the bow slowly lifted out of the water. For a minute the ship stood trembling above the waves. There was a crack like cannon fire and a rush of splintering, and she pitched deep into the oncoming trough. The two men listened. Above were running feet—to the stern. So it was not the mast!

Waxel lifted his arms to the deck above. "Almighty God! Deliver us! Deliver us this once! Bring us out of this storm and we won't go on! We will wait in America! I swear it!" The paroxysm passed in a sob. "Almighty God, help us, help us all."

On October twenty-fourth the wind dropped suddenly and the *St. Peter* sailed in a thick fall of snow. During the night watch this too passed and Khitrov saw the familiar stars turning across the sky as they had always done. He looked back at the first yellow streak of light and watched the sun rise above the horizon and rest for a few moments on the sea. The ship was running before the wind and in the brilliantly beautiful morning the three weeks of storm seemed unreal, like a dream one cannot remember.

By afternoon the grayness had closed round them again. The officers sat in the cabin going over the facts. They had been driven back three hundred miles to the east; it was now late in October and they were more than a thousand miles from Avacha. The brandy and biscuits had given out. The only food on board was a little dried whale meat, some flour, and some fish oil. The water was low, the crew was sick, the rigging rotten.

"We can't go on. That's all."

"Ten men to run the ship!"

"He'll see it when he thinks about it."

"Fifteen casks of water. There's nothing to think about there," Khitrov said.

Waxel gathered up his papers. When he had gone the officers walked about in the cabin restlessly. In their hearts they knew that Waxel would fail, that the Commander would not give in, that he would hold to his purpose to reach Avacha. Is it possible that they felt this because, in their hearts, they also knew that this was the thing which had to be done?

Bering lay in his bed, sunk in the pain and the blackness of scurvy. But the mind which had run so simply that it had seemed stupid to the Academists did not mislead him. Waxel had gone over his evidence. He had reported the whole condition of the ship. But he knew, by the look of patient waiting in the Commander's eyes, that his arguments had had no effect.

"It is impossible for us to go on, sir," he concluded.

"There is nothing else we can do," Bering answered. "We cannot make a landing on this coast and expect to sail again. What food have you for the men? What shelter, on these barren rocks? Our only hope is to reach Avacha. You say that it is impossible, but you cannot know that. You do not know what winds will blow. You do not know what strength remains in the men. To decide that it is impossible to make port, to say that it is useless to go on—that is scurvy speaking, Lieutenant Waxel!"

Waxel returned to the cabin frightened and confused. He sat down at the table without speaking and took out his journal. The officers understood. Betge and Esselberg went to their bunks. After watching the stunned faces around him for a few minutes, Steller too got out some paper and began to write.

Waxel's entry in his journal ran, "On October fifth we came to latitude 51 north. At this place there blew an indescribable gale from the west which continued until October twenty-fourth. During the whole time we had to heave to and were carried to the eastward about eighty Dutch miles." This covered the facts. But this storm had been unusual, and Waxel felt that the facts should be elaborated. He wrote, "In order that the Admiralty College may form some idea of the storm it should be pointed out that old navigators said they had seldom seen anything like it." He remembered the vow he had made and was uneasy. He was not afraid of God at the moment. He was afraid it would be said that he had contemplated mutiny. He concluded his report: "Although on account of the hard labor and continuous inclement weather, we are at the end of our strength, yet with the help of God we will make every effort to reach the Harbor of St. Peter and St. Paul."

But it was not in Waxel's power to hide anything. George Steller saw everything and wrote fluently. He described the storm—the walls of water, the shooting clouds, the noise of the wind in the rigging, the splintering planks, and the screams of the men. He did not spare the officers. "We drifted under the might of God whither the angry heavens willed to send us. No one possessed either courage or council, but the minds of all became as shaky as their teeth." He told of plots to override the Commander, and ended, "But the wind has changed, and with the wind, the officers' determination to winter in America."

Khitrov sat alone at the long side of the table, watching Waxel and Steller write. He too had a journal to keep. He sighed and lifted it out of his coat. He wrote slowly, but had finished first. He noted the position of the ship, the condition of the sails, and the number of the sick. What else was there? He watched the others, wondering what they found to write about, then he bent over his paper and added one of his rare comments, "I have such pains in my feet and hands, owing to the scurvy, that I can with difficulty stand my watch."

Khitrov puzzled over Waxel's failure with the Commander for a week. There wasn't enough water to reach Avacha, and so they had to land. Why were they talking about the rigging and the crew? During that week four men died of scurvy. Three of these were "able-bodied" who fell dead at their posts.

When he had thought about the matter for a week Khitrov went to the Commander with a plain demand for water and accomplished what Waxel had failed to do. He got orders to set the course north for America. The *St. Peter* had been keeping south of Avacha in order to avoid this land which they knew lay to the north of them. They were now to go north, as far as the Avacha parallel, and proceed east at that latitude in order to have an anchorage at hand if the water gave out. The orders were still to sail on—on to Avacha. But in the meantime they were also sailing for the nearest land. The officers believed that water, crew, and ship would give out before they reached Avacha, but they were satisfied.

Steller understood this double purpose better than the officers themselves. He disliked vagueness and divided authority and he disliked everything that Khitrov did. He wrote in his journal, "Under two leaders, betrayed and sold, we proceeded north with the intention of either reaching Kamchatka or stopping at the earliest opportunity at the nearest convenient island. This was proclaimed openly, in order to discourage the sick still more."

They were now sailing north, but this made no change in the world around them. The same green fog rolled about them and the same gray waves rolled toward them from under the mist. They were waiting. Three men died as an uneventful week went by.

On the morning of November eighth the mist thinned ahead and they saw a dark mass of land bearing down on them. The cry from the lookout brought every man to the deck. Unexpected, unfamiliar land is the real danger of the sea. Nothing that wind or water can do has such menace. The cry "Land ahead!" sent every man clambering into the foremast as the ship began to turn into the wind. Almost at once the fog parted and they sailed into open water. The shores of Kiska rose before them, barely a mile away.

Khitrov called for the anchor and the men dropped from the rigging. But before they could loosen the overside ropes Waxel was running forward, shouting to them to stop. He pushed through the men and caught Khitrov by the shoulder.

"What are you doing? Are you crazy?" He struck the master across the chest to take his hand from the rail. "How are you going to get it up?"

Khitrov staggered against the cable and fell, pulling Waxel with him. The two men, weakened by scurvy and overwork, rolled together on the deck, and the crew moved back in fright. But the officers were not fighting. Waxel got to his feet. He lifted Khitrov and tried to speak calmly.

"You are running this ship with ten feeble men, Master Khitrov. Remember that. All of you together couldn't weigh the anchor."

Khitrov was unnerved by what he now considered his mistake. He believed that if the anchor had gone down the ship would have been lost. His huge body ached in every muscle and his mind was blank. Incapable of giving orders, or of thinking at all, he left the deck and somehow found his way to the cabin. He sat looking at the bunks, wondering if the last of the brandy really had been given out.

Meanwhile the southeast wind, which had driven away the fog, caught the sails. The bow swung slowly round to the west and the *St. Peter* moved out to sea. Waxel stood on deck

watching the ship turn off the land and then went below to
tell Khitrov that all was clear.

When he saw the stunned face of the master the words died
in his throat. He said gently, "I suppose you were thinking of
the water?"

"Yes," said Khitrov numbly and without thought. "Yes. We
must get water soon or a great misfortune will overtake us."

Steller's laugh startled the two officers. Neither of them had
seen him until that moment, but he was sitting at the table
near them. He was amused by Khitrov's "great misfortune"
and said bluntly, "We almost found our graves in the water
this day."

Khitrov shuddered. Such words brought misfortune on a
ship. "It is dangerous to go on our way," he said.

The officers had failed at last. The sudden appearance of
land, calling for quick, fateful decisions, had snapped their
nerves, strained by weeks of monotony. They forgot why the
land was there. They forgot everything except the habits
which years of discipline had taught them. They no longer
had the strength to think. The blind courage that was in the
crew was in them too, to a high degree, and kept them at their
work for another four weeks. But more than that was needed
to direct the work.

This island had come to them out of the mist because they
had set their course for it. Their decision of a week before
had not altered the tiny world which centered on them, but it
had determined what chance brought into that world. The
officers should have let the *St. Peter* run on this land if they
still wanted to winter in America. That day they also reached
the parallel of Avacha and should have turned west if they
still hoped to make port. They did neither.

They cleared the land and set the course north again, for no
reason except that that was the course they were sailing. The
St. Peter no longer had a helmsman. She passed north of

Avacha. She passed north of the American islands into the sea beyond. And still she sailed north.

On November fifteenth they were approaching the last island in the Aleutian chain, which lies about a hundred miles off the coast of Kamchatka. During the morning the lookout sighted land, and an hour later it could be seen from the deck. The news that they had reached Avacha gave everyone new strength, and dying men who had not moved for weeks crawled to the deck to see. Some men were praying and some were sobbing like children, realizing for the first time how much they had endured. Then a pale yellow light fell on the ship. The sun was coming through the mist. A chorus of shouts went up from the *St. Peter* as the men forgot the land and turned their faces to the brightening sky above the mast. It was the first sunlight they had had in almost three weeks.

The land they had first sighted now lay south of them about twelve miles; more land could be seen in the west, perhaps twenty miles distant. Waxel brought his maps on deck. What they saw before them corresponded to the maps of Avacha. As the air cleared the resemblance was even greater. They were able to identify certain mountain peaks, and some thought they saw the Vauna lighthouse.

Khitrov had gone to take a noon observation. Two men were letting out a reef in the main topsail. The others lay on the deck in the sun. Waxel stood alone, watching the land, praising God for it. "Not a mile off the course! A thousand navigators could not have hit it off like that. But God has done it. In spite of all I thought, and all I tried to do, the ship has come into Avacha!"

At that moment he heard Khitrov calling. He was running forward along the deck, shouting as he came, and the men were struggling to their feet behind him. Waxel took one

glance at the paper Khitrov was holding and ran to the foresail brace. In a minute everyone knew that they were turning
into the wind to keep off this land, that what a moment ago
had meant home and the end of all danger was now menacing
them.

Waxel felt strong arms take the rope behind him, and
Ovtsin asked, "What is it?"

"We're north of 54–54°30′."

The yard swung slowly into place and Ovtsin did not answer. A hundred miles north of Avacha! And God knows
how far east!

"It's the long time in thick weather with no sun to set us
right," Waxel explained.

The mistake did not have to be explained. An error of a
hundred miles was not much on a three-thousand-mile voyage
through uncharted seas. As a matter of fact, the log for that
day showed their position by dead reckoning as sixty miles
north of Avacha. But they had no faith in their records.

What did need to be explained was this land ahead of them.
Waxel went back to his maps which lay on the deck near
Khitrov's cuddy. They now knew where they were by the
sun—and they were opposite the mouth of the Kamchatka
River. Waxel examined the coast line shown on the map, and
it bore no resemblance to the land before him. But at this
point the sea too had been charted and there were no islands.
Either this was the mainland or they were hopelessly lost at
sea. "It must be Kamchatka," he said aloud.

"It can't be." Ovtsin had followed him and was looking at
the map. "That's where the Commander was in '28. He charted
all of this."

"I didn't ask you." Waxel's voice rose in fury. "What are
you doing here? You are a sailor! Get to your work!"

The wind was from the east, and land lay west and south
of them. All afternoon they worked against the wind, trying

to clear the land hemming them in to the south, the land they had once thought was the entrance to Avacha Bay. By evening the wind had risen to a gale. Through the night they tacked north, fighting this wind which was carrying them on shore. All night the numbed, exhausted men struggled with the foremast sails. They set and reset them but were too weak to take them in. The shrouds snapped and the sails, which could not be reefed, split apart.

The wind went down just before dawn. As the danger and terror lessened, the men dropped. At seven o'clock Khitrov found "eight men, who with great pain can look after themselves, and of these only three can come on deck." The ship was still twenty miles to sea and there was a light onshore breeze.

Waxel and Khitrov went together to the men's quarters. In the half-dark room men were lying on the leather flour sacks and between the barrels of salted whale, whimpering and moaning. Those who were able to get up were expecting the officers and came forward to meet them.

Waxel waited for a few minutes till his eyes adjusted to the darkness. "You know the condition of the ship," he said at last. "The sails are gone on the mainmast and we can't repair it. You know your own condition. The ship is without control. I do not believe we can get around this land to the south, but I believe we can find an anchorage here. Do you want to look for an anchorage, or go on? This is not Avacha. We are north of Avacha about a hundred miles."

"Is this Kamchatka?" someone asked.

"That's Ovtsin's work!" Waxel thought. "The men of themselves would never have questioned it." He answered angrily, "Of course it's Kamchatka! What else could it be?"

Someone else said, "If it's not Kamchatka, we ought to go on."

"I tell you it is! On my honor, this land ahead of us is part of Kamchatka! We can send overland to Avacha and get help."

"If it isn't Kamchatka, you can cut my head off!" Khitrov added.

This seemed to silence the doubters. Someone said, "We can't stay at sea. Who's to handle the ship?"

"Can I tell the Commander that's what you all say—that you all want to anchor here?" Waxel asked.

"Tell him we can't do our work."

"Say there's no able-bodied."

"The lieutenant knows what to say."

Waxel made his way back across the deck, hardly aware of the men who followed him. His mind was on what he had to do. The men crowded into the cabin with him and filled the alley beyond. When he saw the familiar, set look on the Commander's face Waxel's heart sank. He turned angrily on Khitrov. "Can't you keep the men out? Why are they here?" he demanded. But it was too late. The crowded men could not get back easily, and Khitrov knew better than to frighten them at this moment. Bering lay in his bunk. He turned his eyes on the men before him, slowly realizing that the whole crew had come to make a demand.

Waxel had stated his facts. "We have reached the Kamchatka coast a hundred miles north of Avacha," he was saying. "Considering that we have no able-bodied men, that our provisions and water are gone, our rigging rotten——"

"How can you be certain that this is Kamchatka?" Bering asked. "We must try to reach Avacha. We do not know this coast, and it would be unwise to anchor here. We have endured a great deal, I know. But we should not despair. We have risked so much, we must risk a little more."

"We are sick to death, sir!" Waxel cried. "We are at the very end of our strength and in very great danger! We cannot get around this cape while the wind is contrary. And we are giving out so fast we cannot wait for the wind to change."

"All men die in time, Lieutenant Waxel. And sooner or later does not matter much. But if the ship does not reach Avacha it will all have been for nothing."

"Brave words from a dying man!" Waxel cried, losing control of himself. "You—you will keep us at sea till the last man is destroyed by this dreadful disease!"

"What does Ovtsin think?" Bering asked abruptly.

Waxel turned startled eyes on Khitrov. He saw the master lurch into the alley, heard scuffling and then silence. "Ovtsin is not here," he said quietly.

Bering understood. "You are resolved to make a landing here," he said. "And you tell me that you are all of one mind about this. I think you are making a mistake and that much suffering and recrimination will follow. So see to it that everyone signs the petition to land."

The men moved slowly out of the cabin. Waxel pushed his way through them to the officers' quarters where Khitrov was waiting for him. "Good!" he whispered. "Will he sign, do you think?"

"He'll sign anything," Khitrov said.

Waxel moved on toward his bunk. Steller was sitting at the further side of the table, watching them nervously. "You agree with us, don't you?" Waxel asked, catching sight of Steller. "You agree that we can't go further?"

Steller had been preparing his answer to this question. "I am not usually consulted in naval matters," he said. "And as you've told me so often that I know nothing about navigation, I think that now I'd rather say nothing at all."

Waxel understood clearly enough that Steller was refusing to sign. It probably didn't matter whether this man signed or not, he was so peculiar, but trouble could come from strange sources. Waxel tried to speak pleasantly. "As you say, you know nothing about navigation and can't form an opinion on that. But as an intelligent man—you can see the condition the crew is in. Can't you sign a statement to the effect that they aren't able to do their work?"

Steller thought for a moment. "I suppose I can conscientiously sign that," he said.

Waxel slumped into his berth without a word and the same minute rolled onto his back asleep. The problem which had goaded him for eight weeks was silenced at last. He slept heavily, through the day and far into the night. He did not hear the anchors dropped or the feet running above him or Khitrov's screams.

At sundown they were nearing shore. But the moon was bright and they went on. They could see the heavy breakers ahead. After a time black pinnacles of rock showed through the foaming water. When these were half a mile away they dropped anchor.

But they had come too far and were caught in the running tide. The anchor cable snapped without a perceptible tug. The ship swept on into shallow water, carrying them within sound of the surf.

The panic-stricken men stumbled down the deck and heaved the spare anchor. The ship was tossing like a ball, her keel grinding the sandy bottom. The anchor actually spun through the air, and the cable snapped the instant it struck water.

Screams of terror tore from the men as they ran blindly forward to the last anchor, which hung on the port bow. Above the noise of the breakers Khitrov could be heard shouting, "The ship! The ship! A disaster to the ship!"

Then Ovtsin's voice: "Get back! All of you! Stay back!"

He had thrown himself across the capstan to hold them off, but his commanding tone was all they needed. The men fell back, waiting for his orders.

"You lost the others! This is all we've got!" he shouted.

Then he turned his head and looked toward the shore. All eyes followed his. In silent terror they watched the oncoming rocks. The bow pierced the foam. The ship shot into the breakers—and through them.

The sails dropped suddenly, and the *St. Peter* swayed on a placid, windless bay. The men drew in their breath and Ovtsin laughed. He stepped aside, and they let the anchor down in quiet water. The *St. Peter* had come through a narrow channel to the only spot on that entire coast where a ship could ride.

13. SHIPWRECK

IN THE quiet sunny morning the men stood on deck and looked at their surroundings in dismay. The ship lay in a cove less than a mile wide. Before them was a narrow stretch of dunes and beyond this, masses of treeless rock. They heard the thunder of the surf along the rocky shores to the north and to the south of them.

Waxel went ashore to reconnoiter, taking some of the sick with him. He returned to report that there was water but no timber or vegetation of any kind. If this were an island, a wind-swept rock lying in the sea wholly cut off from the post at Avacha, it would be impossible to winter here. And Waxel and Khitrov half knew that it was. But it was just as impossible to get away. Neither the crew nor the ship was equal to the coasts which hemmed them in. Therefore, insisting that this was the mainland, they began to take the sick ashore.

There were still ten "able-bodied." Until now all aboard the *St. Peter* had been bound together in a common fate; the man who died trying to save the ship was doing the only thing he could to save himself. But this was no longer the case. Now anyone able to go ashore could lie down and rest, unaffected by what happened to anyone else. But there were forty-nine men who could not get ashore, who were too sick to save their own lives and who would have to be lifted into the longboat and carried up the sands. The need of these men, like the need of the ship before, kept the half-sick struggling on their feet as long as Khitrov gave the orders.

For these men, taking the longboat ashore often meant wading in icy sea water up to their shoulders. Sometimes they brought the boat back the same day with a load of fresh water. Sometimes they made two trips in one day. And sometimes they were too exhausted to remember anything and the boat would not return for several days. At such times flags were run up on the *St. Peter*, signaling for them to come, reminding them that there was no drinking water on board.

The sick were disturbed and made worse by being moved. They lay on the sands, without covering, without knowing where they were, crying like children. The mouths of many were so badly affected by scurvy that they could not swallow, "the gums swollen like a sponge, brown black, grown over the teeth and covering them." Out of these mouths men cried for their mothers, whimpering that they were hungry or thirsty or cold.

As soon as the bodies were laid on the sands arctic foxes swarmed over them. So far there had been nothing on this island that killed for food, and none of the animals knew fear. The great sea mammals lived on fish or grass. The foxes were so much smaller than anything else on the island that they had to live on carrion. Every morning they came down from the rocks and ran among the sleeping herds, sniffing at each animal to see if it were still alive and dragging away whatever was dead.

When Bering's men came from the sea and lay down on the sands, the foxes treated them as they did every other herd. Some of the sick breathed so feebly that the foxes bit their ears to make sure they were alive. The instant the first man died the foxes knew it and rushed together to devour the body. This mutilation of the corpse horrified the dying men more than death itself. They fought off the foxes with their hands while a grave was quickly dug. Then they dug more graves in anticipation, getting them ready for sick men who had not yet been brought ashore.

The last of the men were taken from the ship on November twenty-fifth. Seven were carried on that trip and four died while being moved. The next day Khitrov came ashore. Some men still lay on the beach; some had been moved into trenches which were covered with sailcloth. Over them all the wind whistled louder than the pounding surf. On all sides there was nothing but treeless rock.

Khitrov, used to the narrow, cramped cabin, was terrified by the exposure, the complete lack of wood for walls. "We can't do this! We can't stay here!" he said to Waxel.

"Where shall we go?"

"The ship. There's more warmth and comfort in the ship. It would be better to stay there."

Both men looked at the *St. Peter* and at the reefs beyond. She was held by a single cable and could not long remain where she was.

Khitrov answered the unspoken thought: "We could go beyond the reef and anchor out at sea," adding hopelessly, "When we are able."

Waxel spoke dully. Neither he nor Khitrov believed what he said. "We can send to Avacha, when we are able."

After the anchor had gone down on the *St. Peter*, on the night of November sixteenth, George Steller decided that the ship would not hold together much longer and went below and packed his things. He and sixty-three others had just escaped death in a most dramatic manner, and it occurred to him that his notebooks were in danger. When morning came and he called Thomas to carry his sacks on deck he had more than two hundred pounds of luggage he was taking with him. Fortunately for him, Waxel was in charge. Khitrov would never have allowed the bags to go ashore. But Waxel was too exhausted, too conscious of all that had to be done before his strength gave out, to waste any of it in fight.

"That weighs more than a man," he said, looking at the bags.

"What can I do?" Steller asked. "I can't come back to the ship for it. I can't leave it behind."

Waxel cut him short. "Put it in. We're going."

There were sixty-four men aboard ship on the morning of November seventeenth. Khitrov lists forty-nine sick and ten able-bodied, which leaves five unaccounted for. Perhaps all of these were men who could take care of themselves but were of no use to anyone else, and went ashore with Waxel along with the sick. Certainly there were three such men in the boat —Steller, his servant Thomas, and a German soldier, Frederic Plenisner.

Plenisner was able-bodied enough. He could hunt and dig and carry driftwood. But in the weeks which followed he was at Steller's disposal and not Khitrov's. Steller, who wished to give him as much dignity as he could, says that he was a surveyor. But he was extraordinarily stupid and never said anything that Steller could quote beyond the recurring, "Mr. Plenisner agreed with me in this."

Steller addressed several remarks to Plenisner while they were in the boat, and the soldier agreed with everything he said. Finding him such pleasant company, Steller suggested that they have tea together as soon as they reached land.

Plenisner agreed that tea would be nice and was told to build up a fire and get the water ready.

Plenisner doubtless imagined that the doctor had some tea. But Steller intended to find it among the rocks while his companion brought the water to a boil. He climbed a hillock and looked about him. What he saw confirmed what he already thought. He says that he saw sea sky in the west. Perhaps he did. Perhaps the sky beyond gave him such solid evidence that he would have known he was on an island even if he had previously supposed it was the mainland. But it was evidence that Waxel and Khitrov could not credit.

Steller returned to Plenisner with his news and with some wintergreen which he brewed into tea. It was the first warm food either of them had had in weeks. It would have tasted good if it had been merely hot water, and Steller's tea was certainly more nourishing than that.

"I am afraid we are on an island," he said.

Plenisner held the steaming cup under his face and answered, "I wouldn't like to say that for sure."

"You say that because you don't want to discourage me," Steller replied. It was the first contradiction he had had from Plenisner. "But we must not lull ourselves with pretty dreams! We will have to spend the winter here, and we should think about some kind of shelter. We should build a hut from driftwood."

"A hut would be a good thing," said Plenisner. "But first we ought to eat."

"That is true! If you will find the meat for our meal I will find the salads and learn more about our surroundings. We can return to this spot in a couple of hours. Are you sure you have your bearings and can find the place again?"

Plenisner did not take offense. He said he was certain he could find his way back and that he would bring fresh meat with him.

Steller and Thomas went inland, through narrow gorges where the wind blew so strong they could scarcely keep their feet. Its whistling rose above the roar of the sea which still sounded in their ears. Here, where other men saw nothing, Steller found several kinds of edible leaves and berries. He also saw that the vegetation was Siberian and not American.

"This island we are on is very near Kamchatka," he told Thomas. "You see these plants are just as you have always known them. There's nothing peculiar about any of them." He handed the servant some leaves to put in his sack.

Thomas had seen nothing peculiar about the plants in America; it had all looked just like Kamchatka to him. He examined the leaves in his hand thoughtfully, but his mind was on something else. What his master said about their being near Kamchatka was no consolation to him. If this horrible place was an island, they would have to stay here all winter, so what difference did it make where it was? This wasn't the job he had been hired for, and what sort of pay was he going to get in a place like this? He threw the leaves on the ground.

"What do I get for serving you?" he asked. "We are all going to starve on these rocks. And you brought me here! It is not my occupation to go to sea. I would never have come on this voyage except for you."

"Thomas! Don't blame me for your misfortunes! Do you know all that would have happened to you by now if you had stayed at home? And you will not starve as long as you are with me."

Thomas wiped his eyes. "I could have had good times this winter on the Bolshaya River."

At that moment they were surrounded by a pack of arctic foxes, half of which had blue pelts. The arctic fox is normally white, and the blue color is an abnormality due to faulty diet. This fur was highly prized during the eighteenth and nineteenth centuries. At least a third of the foxes on this island had the precious, blue-tinted coats. The little animals ran around the men like dogs, sniffing their hands and trying to chew their bootstraps. That anything with such dangerously precious fur existed in large numbers proved to Steller that no Siberian fur trader had ever set foot here.

Thomas lost his head at the sight of so much wealth and swung about him with his ax, killing eight blue foxes in as many minutes. The little dead bodies which he piled under a ledge of rock represented more than he could earn by many years of hard labor. He only needed to skin them and turn them over to a trader.

The island had lost most of its bleakness for Thomas, and he obediently followed Steller through the ravines, carrying his bags. They reached the sea a mile south of the bay in which the *St. Peter* lay at anchor. Here there were no dunes. Milk-white water pounded against rocks. The waves rose to such incredible heights that for a minute both men watched the sea in terror. Then they turned away. A short distance from them were dry rocks, and on these lay a herd of seal-like animals.

Otters! Neither man could believe his eyes. Steller did not earn the equivalent of three sea-otter skins a year, and more than a hundred of these animals now lay on the rocks before them. They were playing with their young and caressing one another in perfect security. Nothing had ever frightened them here.

The two men approached the herd cautiously. Steller, intent on what he saw, forgot about Thomas, and Thomas, seeing thousands of rubles within reach, forgot about his master. When they were a few feet from the nearest animal he jumped forward with a terrible yell and struck it with the blunt side of the ax. The otter screamed and the whole herd rose in alarm and slid into the water. The glossy black fur lay loose on their bodies, rippling like velvet as they ran. Steller watched a female take her suckling young in her mouth and drive a half-grown cub before her into the sea. The bull, an animal five feet long and weighing over sixty pounds, faced the intruders and moved backward to the sea, blowing and hissing like an angry cat. The animal which had been struck was cut off from the herd by the two men. As the ax rose again it cowered, covering its eyes with its forefeet. When struck it relaxed in death, rolling onto its back and crossing the forefeet on its breast. The humanlike gesture terrified Thomas and he stepped back. But in a minute he recovered himself, remembered the value of what he had got, and lifted the precious burden to his back.

They went back to the *St. Peter*, following the shore. The otters from a safe distance in the water were watching them, holding their feet above their eyes to shade them from the sun. They stood upright like men, jumping up and down with the waves, and scolding or jeering. A female came out of the water alone and climbed over the rocks to the place where she had lost her cub, crying bitterly in an almost human voice.

Coming on a sheltered spot where weed and sand had accumulated, Steller found a half-buried piece of wood which he recognized as part of a shutter such as the Russians used in Kamchatka. This merely bore out what he already knew from the vegetation—that they were not far from the mainland. Lifting the shutter, he saw something under it and knew at once that it was important. It was a piece of shell, and so important that he sat down to think clearly, turning it over in his hands. It was man-made, for a purpose. It was a trap. It was made by people who did not have metal, by Americans, not Siberians. Therefore the American coast was not far away either.

In order to start this chain of reasoning Steller had to overlook the fact that this shell was so brittle that it would not serve as a trap; no one would have used it for a trap. Steller had found a toy which an Eskimo child had lost in the sea, a plaything made to resemble their traps of walrus ivory. It was too precious to hand over to Thomas, and he placed it carefully inside his coat.

As they were approaching the beach Steller made another discovery. Here arms of rock ran into the sea for several hundred yards, with pools of semisheltered water between them. In one of these they came on a herd of enormous animals which were browsing under water. The rise and fall of the waves never completely uncovered them, and Steller could see only their backs and heads. The backs, which were more than twenty feet long, rose in a hump with hollows on either side like an ox. They were grazing like land cattle, with a slow forward movement, tearing the seaweed from the rocks at their feet, chewing ceaselessly, concerned with nothing but their food. Every few minutes they lifted buffalolike heads and drew in air with a rasping, snorting sound.

Steller had never seen or heard of anything like this. He caught his servant's arm. "Look, Thomas! What is that animal? What do you call it in Kamchatka?"

"I don't know!" Thomas was frightened. "What is it doing under the water? What is it?"

"Thomas! Do the Kamchatkans call this *makoai?*"

"No! No! There's nothing like this in Kamchatka!"

This was what Steller most wanted to hear, but he had to press his point. He knew that the words he used were supposed to apply to whales, but this animal might be known to the natives of the mainland and referred to by them under one of these names. "Isn't it called *plebun?*"

Thomas' fright was increased by his master's foolish questions. He pointed a trembling hand at the snorting beasts before them. "That's not a fish!" he gasped.

Thomas had acquired eight blue foxes and a sea otter within two hours and was a very happy man. But Steller had found something infinitely more precious than fur. He had found an unknown species of animal which he would be able to observe all winter. Both men were pleased with the fate which had cast them on these rocks. Thomas overestimated his good fortune. While they remained on this island the furs were worth less than the shoe leather consumed in going after them. But Steller's good fortune was even greater than he supposed. He was not only the discoverer of these animals, he was to be the only trained observer, the only scientist, to ever see them. By the time his reports reached civilization and other men came to study the thing he called a sea cow, the whole species had been exterminated.

This twenty-ton animal was one of Life's mistakes. Like the birds, and unlike any other animal, it had only two feet. These were under the chest and resembled the hoofs of horses. With these the animal pawed the seaweed from the rocks. The animal had no fins of any kind. Below the navel was an enormous tail consisting entirely of fat. The sea cow could not move its great bulk except in water, and it could not swim. It kept at one depth, moving in and out with the tide, bound through all time to the shores of this one island.

When Steller and Thomas reached camp Plenisner had already built up a fire. His day had not been as exciting as theirs, but his wants were simple. He had half a dozen ptarmigans and a sealskin. He considered this place no worse than a lot of other places he had been.

Steller looked at the birds and empty skin. "You have kept the brass and thrown away the gold," he said severely. "Where did you leave the animal?"

"It's a little way back," Plenisner answered vaguely.

"You must get it," said Steller. "But we will have our meal first. Ptarmigans are pleasant food for men who need nothing, and I will make soup of them tomorrow. But if we are not to all die of scurvy, we must eat red meat and animal fat."

He was already cutting up Thomas' otter, and in a short time three pieces of meat were broiling in the fire. Steller knew the medicinal value of this food so well that he actually tasted its virtues when he bit into the rank-smelling flesh.

"What a wonderful flavor!" he exclaimed. "Have you tasted it yet, Mr. Plenisner?"

Plenisner was just tasting it, and worse-tasting food he had never put in his mouth. But he saw fit to swallow it without protest. Tomorrow he would have ptarmigan, boiled greens, and peas if he took his medicine now. Thomas disliked the meat too, but he was used to eating whatever was given him without a murmur.

"Through the flesh of sea animals God will strengthen us, who have come to grief through the sea," Steller said devoutly.

At that minute a blue fox ran from among their bags with two ptarmigans. Thomas yelled and Plenisner jumped up, but the animal got away. They put the rest of their meat in bags and brought them close to the fire.

Tea was ready. This time it was brewed from cranberry leaves. The three men, unaccustomedly full of food, dozed beside the fire and sipped their tea in stupefied content. Thomas soon rolled over asleep. On the sands below, the boat had come ashore again with more of the sick. Reminded of the *St. Peter* and his old grievances, Steller explained to Plenisner the mistakes in judgment, the weaknesses in character, which had brought them and the whole ship to this pass. Plenisner agreed with him completely. In all Steller's extraordinary journal there is no statement more astonishing than his entry of November seventeenth, where he tells how he and Mr. Plenisner, within sight of the sick, sat down by a stream and "regaled ourselves with tea, at the same time remembering the unjust conduct of various people."

While they were so occupied one of these people joined them. Waxel was returning from exploring the island and

came to the only fire on the beach. Steller saw that he was
sick and faint and gave him tea. Waxel accepted it thankfully.
Holding his hands on the warm cup, he looked dully at the
half-naked men on the sands below.

Steller had a great deal he wanted to say. "God knows
whether this is Kamchatka!" he began.

Waxel started out of his reverie. "Of course it's Kamchatka! It couldn't be anything else!"

"I don't know about that. It doesn't look like Kamchatka
to me. The great number and tameness of the animals suggests an uninhabited island. But I would say that we are not
far from Kamchatka. The plants here occur in the same number, proportion, and size as in Kamchatka, while the peculiar
plants discovered in America are not found here at all." His
words flowed on—sea sky—Russian shutter—American trap.
"All of this seems to me to prove that we are on an island
which is in a narrow channel between the Siberian and American coasts."

Waxel could not follow the words. Nothing this man said
had any sense to it. These waters had been explored by competent seamen. There was no narrow channel here, or body
of land to the east. But this man had spent the day turning
over leaves and driftwood, spinning fantastic thoughts and
drawing conclusions which would demoralize the whole
ship's company!

Waxel got to his feet. He waved his arm toward the men
on the beach and spoke excitedly. "Those things aren't important. This is no time to speculate. We must look after the
men. We must get them covered!"

Seeing that the lieutenant would leave at once, Plenisner
took two ptarmigans from the bag. He knew the value of the
birds and how they should be treated. "Will you give these
to the Commander with my compliments?" he asked.

"Oh yes," said Steller. "And some salads too, Mr. Plenisner. They are important. And some sea-otter meat." He turned to the lieutenant. "Urge the Commander in every way to eat this rather than the ptarmigan. It is delicious!"

Waxel made his report to the Commander, and Bering understood him only too well—the anchor was down and could not be raised; the disabled men were going ashore. The ship would probably be lost, and this was not Kamchatka! The blind, stubborn strength which had carried him so far snapped under the blow. His body sank limply in the bed. "We are in God's hands!" he said helplessly.

But this was immediately followed by the thought "We always were." Bering gave a faint gasp of surprise. For ten years he had struggled alone, believing desperately that it rested with him alone whether or not the labor of a thousand lives should come to nothing. And suddenly the world of striving had slipped from him and he looked down the long vistas of Quiet. Others who have endured beyond the limits of humankind have seen that same world, but it lies outside language. All that we who live in struggle can know is that it is a re-evaluation of life and that it is accompanied by an intense awareness of the physical world—the splendor of the grass and the glory of the flower. Bering laughed softly. It was so astonishing, so obvious, so simple! How absurd that he hadn't known it all his life!

"All my life has been in fog," he thought. "But now God has driven it away."

Betge, sitting in the cabin in blank terror, heard the low, happy laugh and looked at the Commander. He saw the satisfaction and contentment in his face. Until that moment he had stayed with the Commander out of duty, but from then on he clung to him. That serene smile warmed him and gave him the only comfort he knew. He never wondered what had given the dying man this calm assurance; it was enough for

him that he had it. When Khitrov offered to send him ashore
ahead of Bering, he shook his head and explained in a whis-
per, "It's a privilege to know a man like that."

On the afternoon of the second day Bering was taken
ashore. With him were his two servants, the surgeon Betge,
and the sailor Ovtsin. Bering was taken to Steller's hut and
laid on the ground. Betge and Ovtsin then covered him with a
sail.

Steller had spent the day building a hut. Driftwood was
hard to find on the island, and Plenisner and Thomas had
followed the shore for several miles before they got as much
as they needed. Steller saw that the rough boards would not
keep out the wind without considerable mortaring, and
warm-pelted foxes were scurrying about on all sides. He cut
a strip of meat from the sea otter and held it in his hand. The
foxes at once swarmed around him, yelping for the food,
while he struck them down with an ax. Within three hours he
had seventy blue skins from which he made a roof for the
hut. When the walls had been set up he filled the holes and
cracks with the bodies of other foxes, which lay around him
in heaps.

Steller saw the extraordinary calm in the Commander's
face and was annoyed by it. Peace was so alien to his nature
that he could see it only as ignorance. When Betge left his
charge to prepare a supper, Steller felt it his duty to explain
the situation to the dying man. He went over his evidence—
sky, plants, animals, shell. A light snow had begun to fall.
Flakes glistened in the old man's hair which lay against the
sand and gradually whitened the sail which covered him.

Bering, content with the world, content with death, was
acutely aware of the majestic beauty around him. The sky
and the sea, the clouds and the rocks were glorious and satis-
fying beyond anything he had ever accomplished in life. He
looked up at Steller while he talked and felt a wondering pity

for this racked, anxious man who stood in the midst of grandeur and did not see it.

The puzzled, kindly expression in the Commander's eyes disturbed Steller. His argument faltered. He said abruptly, "I hope you are eating the sea otter. It is wonderfully nourishing food."

The disturbing look vanished in a smile of simple amusement. "It might be wonderfully nourishing, if I could bring myself to swallow it! Your taste is wonderfully adaptable, Mr. Steller. I marvel at you!"

Steller was unused to compliments of any kind, and this was on a trait which he valued highly in himself. He was greatly moved. For a moment there was a surge of affection in his heart. "I marvel at you, Captain Bering. Such singular contentment—in the face of everything!"

"There is no fog here. That is very strange!" Bering said.

Steller was aware of it for the first time. There had been no fog the two days they had been on the island.

"The fog has great power to hinder us and make us suffer," Bering went on. "It destroys each of us at last; singly, we are all defeated. But it is a passive thing, Mr. Steller. Anything we win from it is won forever. And so we cannot lose. Nothing is ever lost. And I know that we have done a great deal."

Steller understood the Commander but did not agree with him. He smiled at the bleak earth they had won from the foggy waters.

"We have found an unknown island for our graves," he said.

Betge had just finished roasting a ptarmigan when Steller sat down beside him.

"Would you like to join our little group?" he asked, waving his hand toward the hut which Plenisner and Thomas were reinforcing with sand. "You should be thinking of how you are going to live on these rocks, because we will be here a long time."

Betge put down his pan of meat. His mouth opened but he could not speak. This strange, terrible Steller was offering him, a nobody, his house—the only house on the island, the only fire, the only wholesome food. There was no sense to it! He stammered out a frantic acceptance. "It is a great honor! A very great honor. Of course it is more than an honor —it is perhaps my life. I will do everything I can. There are many things I can do if you will only direct me——"

"We can work out the housekeeping details later. There is plenty of time," said Steller. "But first you should have rest. I will show you where you can sleep."

A terror seized Betge. He was prepared to pay almost any price for this protection in the way of cringing or flattery. But there was one price he could not pay. "The Commander," he stammered. "I cannot leave him. It's my duty, as surgeon, you know."

Steller was gracious. "As you think best," he said. "It won't be for long."

That night the wind rose to a gale and the hut which had looked so solid in the gently falling snow went down like a house of twigs. Leaving Thomas to catch their cups and pans, Steller and Plenisner ran after the fur roof which rolled ahead of them across the sands. They had run half a mile before they caught hold of it. A few minutes later, struggling back against the wind and blinding sand, they both fell head-long into a grave which had been dug for two bodies.

Here there was no wind. "This is wonderful!" said Steller before Plenisner could get his breath. "This is just what we want! Get Thomas and bring everything here. We will make this place perfect tomorrow."

Before daylight they had the roof securely fastened down over the pit and a driftwood fire burning at the open end.

The three men sat crouched on their supply sacks. Steller told them that they were very comfortable, and they were indeed warm. But they were painfully cramped. For the next hour Steller gave Plenisner directions for improving their home—it must be dug broader and longer and deeper and lined with driftwood. In the growing light he saw a doubtful, almost sulky expression on Mr. Plenisner's face. He laughed. "I don't expect you to do it all yourself. I will get some cossacks to help you."

At noon the German constable Roselius and the Russian boatswain Ivanov, who had begun the grave, came to finish their work. They found the soldier Plenisner overseeing three men who were scooping up sand with cooking pots. At the far end of the pit George Steller was making soup of beach peas and seal oil. Near them lay the Commander with the surgeon Betge sitting beside him like a mournful dog. Betge had spent the morning looking for Steller and when he found him had carried the Commander across the dunes. He now sat watching the work, exhausted but content.

"That's the thing!" said Roselius after his first gasp of surprise. "That's what we want! We'll dig in the sick before we bring any more ashore."

The two officers had shovels, and before night they had almost finished the trench which was later known as the barracks. Steller spent the afternoon over his soup, but from time to time he came to look at the digging. At dusk when they were preparing to stop he said to Roselius, "Would you like to eat with us?" Roselius and Ivanov looked at each other. He had asked only one of them. Ivanov turned away as if he had not heard.

"Certainly!" said Roselius. "Certainly I would like to taste your soup."

In Steller's pit he found Betge and Plenisner sitting by the fire. In the darkness under the roof were the three servants.

They apparently ate at second table! "A queer lot!" Roselius thought. "But they have food."

The bowls were passed in silence. Roselius swallowed a mouthful and was surprised. "That's extraordinarily good!" he exclaimed.

Steller was pleased. "It is indeed, Mr. Roselius. And it will do extraordinary things for you. We have quite a degree of comfort here." He indicated the dark interior of the dugout. "If you care to join us, we should be glad of your company."

The offer surprised Roselius as much as it had Betge, but he accepted it calmly. "That's fine!" he said. "I'd like that. I'd like nothing better."

"Then it's settled. I will go mark out our sleeping places." Steller took a brand from the fire and disappeared under the roof.

Betge smiled at Roselius timidly. "I'm glad you're going to be one of us," he said, anxious to show that he was one of them and not a chance visitor. "I'm not sleeping in our dugout at present. I feel I must stay with the Commander through the night. But I am on hand all day if there is anything to be done."

"I could use some sleep," Roselius said, peering into the shelter. "But I can't give time during the day. We've twenty men aboard ship without drinking water. And no place to put those on shore."

By the first of December the men had all been brought ashore and laid in the trenches. These were roofed with sails. The men, half naked in their tattered clothing, lay on the ground, covered with rags, wailing and cursing senselessly. Their bodies heated the crowded trench. The filthy clothing which had become wet in the sea or snow steamed on them, mingling its smell with the horrible stench of scurvy. Out in the bay the *St. Peter* rode at anchor without a man on board, her masts and shrouds sheeted with ice.

Khitrov stirred with the first light of day. To the ever-present ache of his sick body was added the stiffness of a night on wet ground and the fatigue of a light sleep. His nights were spent waiting for day, conscious every hour of the slow movement of the stars across the sky. He saw Betge leave the Commander's "tent" and go into Steller's dugout. Soon he saw the smoke of their morning fire. No fire had been lighted yet in the barracks, but with the first restless stirrings of day a chorus of complaining voices began to rise above the solitary moans of the night. After a time Roselius climbed out of Steller's pit and started toward the barracks.

Khitrov was waiting for this. He bent his stiff joints pain-fully and pulled himself to his feet. Roselius stopped in sur-prise.

"Have you had breakfast?" Khitrov asked.

"Yes. . . . Why are you here?"

"I want to show you." Khitrov put his hand on Roselius' arm and went with him to the barracks.

Roselius knew the rotting flesh, the delirious crying of those trenches. But he was not prepared for what he saw. When Khitrov's giant form silhouetted in the entrance the noises changed. The wailing and moaning and random curs-ing gave place to sharp screams of anger. "There he is! . . . You lied to us! . . . Kill him! . . . You stranded us! . . . You've killed us!" The prostrate men half rose among their rags, shaking their arms, crawling a few steps toward the en-trance. Khitrov was not afraid of physical hurt from any of these men. But as the waves of hatred broke around him his whole body shook.

Roselius pulled him back, away from the trench. "You can't go in!" he said, trembling himself.

"No." Khitrov was still dazed by the cries of the men.

"Out here"—he moved his arm—"I lose my strength." His voice rose. "It drains out of me! The ground draws it out! . . . Can you tell him? If he'll take me in for just a little while, I only need a little time. If I could get some sleep I'd mend."

"Yes." Roselius cut him short. "I'll tell him. I'll do what I can. But he's very queer," he added doubtfully.

Roselius left Khitrov and went back to the dugout. He found everyone still at the fire and sat down himself. "I have just seen Master Khitrov," he began. "He is sleeping in the open because it is impossible for him to stay in the barracks."

"I don't doubt it," Steller said placidly. "He is the cause of all our misfortune, and the men would hardly make it pleasant for him. I suppose they reproach him for past doings and make all sorts of threats. I can't say I blame them."

"For God's sake!" Roselius shouted, surprised into anger. "What has that to do with anything? The man will die of exhaustion!" He saw Plenisner smile and Betge lift startled eyes and at once regretted his tone. He could lose all that he had in that shelter without gaining anything for Khitrov. He said quietly, "If we can help him by giving him a corner, don't you think we should?"

"No, I don't think so," said Steller. He was not in the least angry. "We must think of ourselves too. We have an arrangement here which has resulted in cheerfulness and good feeling among us and in our having greater abundance of better-prepared food than anyone else. If we admit such a person as Khitrov we will bring discord on ourselves and destroy all that we have built up. I think we should refuse him absolutely —especially as he is mostly sick from laziness. Tell him that we have discussed it and that we refuse him unanimously."

Roselius left Steller's dugout very uncomfortable about his own position in it. He understood why Plenisner had such a comfortable place. And Betge? Betge was a good sort, but colorless. He would never give offense to anyone. He had probably been civil to this Steller when no one else was, and was getting his reward. But why was Boris Roselius getting so much? Roselius did not feel contemptuous of Steller. But these dependents! An uneasy fear came over him. Was there something marked about him, some outstanding weakness that classed him with a frightened incompetent and a useless toady? Did everyone except himself know what it was?

Khitrov was waiting for him. Roselius shook his head without speaking and went on to the barracks to prepare food.

For the next few days Khitrov did nothing. He slept in the sun and believed he gained more strength each day than he lost each night. But he could not rest. The ship still tossed in the bay, held by a single cable. To Khitrov the ship was more precious than the men, and until the ship was beached he was still on duty. He still kept his journal, but the entries had dwindled to short cries of despair. "At high tide the ship should be drawn up on the beach and made fast with hawsers." "Today I am quite ill and can barely stand on my feet." "Today I am so ill I cannot stand for any reason." "The ship lies out in the open sea and if a strong wind should come up the anchor would not hold." "Something must be done at once because of the winds which may cause us to lose both ship and supplies."

On December seventh Khitrov pulled himself together for a last desperate effort and called for men to beach the ship. The response was five "able-bodied" who followed him across the sands to the longboat. They stooped together to slide it to the water, but it did not move. For a moment they thought it had been weighted down, but as it gave a few inches at a time they realized that it was their own arms and backs which had become incredibly weak. Straining, stumbling, their hands weakening and slipping, they dragged it forward. When the bow struck water there was a sudden lurch. The foremost man, the Koriak interpreter, fell on his face. He made no attempt to get up, but lay sobbing on the sand as the icy waves washed over him. The others pulled him back and then stood looking at the *St. Peter.*

The sea rolled its tireless waves between them and the ship. They knew that they could not hold the oars against it. What would the combined strength of their trembling bodies do against the anchor? The *St. Peter* was tugging at her cable and beyond lay the reefs. In imagination Khitrov saw the anchor raised, or the cable cut, and the ship now straining toward the rocks swept down upon them and dashed to pieces.

"Go back," he said listlessly.

The men pulled the Koriak to his feet and watched the master as he walked away from them across the dunes. Through their pain and exhaustion they looked to him for orders. His faltering steps, the hopeless stoop of his broad back now told them, "Rest. There is nothing more. Rest."

Khitrov stumbled blindly on. His hands had let go the ship. He had given her up. Nothing else mattered. He walked blindly into the barracks. He heard the cries that greeted him. But they did not matter. He lay down and abandoned himself to pain. The throbbing of his body mingled the cries and curses of the men in a delirium. Presently he heard a gale blowing through these sounds and drowning them. The ship was calling to him in great distress. He heard her creaking planks and straining masts, the shriek and moan of her rigging. But he could not move.

That night a strong wind blew onshore. The *St. Peter* leaped and pulled at her cable like a chained animal. Before dawn the frayed rope gave and she was free. She ran high up on the beach, till the sea fell away under her. Then she crashed down, masts and deck striking the earth, and the sea poured over her, filling her hull with sand.

On the morning of December eighth Roselius stepped from

the dugout and saw the *St. Peter*, which had come ashore after them like a faithful dog. She lay a few hundred yards beyond the barracks, buried in the sand. Rigging, decks, and half the hull rose before him, a glistening mass of ice.

14. WINTER

WINTER on Commander Island was a succession of violent winds and blizzards. Snow sometimes lay ten feet on the level ground and the narrow valleys among the rocks filled to the top with drifts. Driftwood was hard to find, and by Christmas Bering's men were carrying their fuel seven and eight miles. The migratory birds soon left, and the sea otter, which at first no one but Steller had been able to eat, became their chief food.

In the weeks immediately following the wreck of the *St. Peter* and the complete collapse of her crew a few men died, altogether six men in six weeks. Among these was the aged Esselberg. The others gradually regained their strength. As the delirium and the weeping passed and the men became conscious of their surroundings, they concentrated their fury on the foxes.

These animals, perhaps because they lived on carrion, had a smell which was worse than that of ordinary foxes, and which nauseated even men who lived in the barracks. And they swarmed everywhere, running over the sleeping men and sniffing at their nostrils to see if they were alive. A man could not skin a sea otter without stabbing several foxes who were trying to tear the meat from his hands. At night the men slept on newly killed otters to protect them, only to find

in the morning that the foxes had eaten away the meat and
entrails from under them. No one could relieve himself without a club in his hand, and the foxes at once ate up the excre-
ment. When a fox found something he had no use for—a
piece of cloth or metal—he befouled it, as if he found de-
struction humorous.

The men forgot the price of these blue pelts. Sometimes
they would dig a ditch and throw in a sea otter and, as the
foxes swarmed in after it, club them to death by the dozen.
But this methodical killing did not satisfy the men's frantic
hate for these animals. They went to great lengths to catch
them alive in order to torture them. Some they strung up in
pairs to bite each other; others they flogged to death. They
burned off one or two legs, gouged out the eyes, or half
skinned them, and then let them run away as an example to
the others. But nothing that happened to one fox made any
impression on another, and they could not be taught fear.
They continued their ravenous attack on the men and their
supplies, even when the packs included several members
missing a leg.

Sea otters were plentiful at first. Herds were found within
a mile of camp, and the animals were so fearless that the men
could walk among them in full daylight without frightening
them away. But, unlike the foxes, they learned fear very
quickly. Perhaps it was because they were very intelligent,
perhaps because they lived in families. At any rate, as the
men grew stronger and more of them went hunting, the otter
moved farther and farther away. Within thirty miles of camp,
both to the north and to the south, cliffs of sheer rock rose
out of the sea, and it was impossible to follow the coast further. By March the sea otter had retreated beyond these walls
and could not be found at all.

In January, however, they were still within five miles of
camp. They came ashore to sleep and play, lying on the rocks

at low tide and moving back to the snow-covered earth as
the tide came in. But they kept close to the water and came
ashore cautiously, looking about them and turning their noses
in all directions to catch a scent. They posted watchers while
they slept and slept lightly. At the slightest noise they would
jump up in fright and go back to the sea. Only a mother who
had lost her young knew no fear. She would remain on shore,
seeking it, crying for it, in the face of any danger. But such
animals did not eat and after a short time would be very sick
and not fit for food.

The men now hunted only on moonless nights and prefer-
ably in a blustering wind. The hunters went out in groups of
three or four, armed with long poles. They crept along the
beaches, keeping against the wind. When a herd of otter was
found one man moved forward to the victim while the others
cut off its approach to the sea. When he was within striking
distance the hunter clubbed the animal on the head, shouting
to the others who closed in on it. The struck animal was
forced to run inland, and so was certain to be caught and
killed eventually.

As this meat became harder to get, the men faced the
prospect of having to eat the foxes. But it did not come to
that. It is difficult for men to eat vermin, and these foxes were
particularly loathsome. Their smell was nauseating and their
color repulsive. The men ate carrion instead, and struggled
with the foxes for it. The foxes could see food quicker than
the men, and when a dead sea otter washed ashore the foxes
would have half devoured it before the men got to it. Many
dead things were washed ashore—otters, sea lions, and fur
seals. Some of these were better than others. Once the sea
brought them "a quite fresh whale," and the camp overflowed
with "comfort and encouragement."

Some sacks of flour were dug out of the *St. Peter's* hull
and made into biscuit to supplement the meat diet. Steller

says, "We were unfortunate in that the flour had been lying pressed hard in leather sacks for two or three years, and at the stranding of the ship had been impregnated with substances dissolved in the salt water, particularly gunpowder, to such a degree that in eating it one did not dare consult one's taste. Until we got used to it our bodies became distended like drums from flatulence."

On the morning of December nineteenth Betge came into the dugout a little before daybreak. He stood silhouetted against the opening, peering into the blackness under the roof.

"What is it?" Steller asked.

"The Commander is dead," he said.

The men got up quickly and climbed out onto the sands. It was a clear, moonless night filled with glittering stars. At their feet lay a dark heap of canvas that was the Commander. Across the gray sand glimmered the hull of the *St. Peter*, and beyond was the white line of the surf. There was nothing for them to do, and they went back to the dugout and waited for day.

With the first blue light they went out again. The news had reached the barracks and the men were already gathering around the corpse. They stared at one another without speaking and moved around aimlessly. Too sick and numb to care about anything, the men were nevertheless conscious of a loss. They realized, with a vague feeling of fright, that the power which had directed them was gone and they were left milling against each other. Steller was the only man on the island who did not realize this. Steller had not seen the fog, he had not seen the strength and courage in the grimy men around him, and he had never known that they had a leader.

The sun had risen and shone warmly on their hands and faces by the time the grave was dug. The diggers came to lift the body. As they drew back the canvas Steller gasped. The body had sunk deeply into the sand. The men shoveled this off with their hands, digging out the corpse in order to bury it.

"At first I kept it off," Betge explained. "But then he asked me to leave it because it helped keep him warm."

They carried the body to its grave and then hesitated before starting to cover it, looking at Steller.

"Will you speak for him?" Betge asked.

Steller nodded. He was confused and curiously disturbed. Standing under a cold, cloudless sky, surrounded by barren rocks and sea, he thought of Moscow—the music, the lights and flowers, the glory and intoxication of the Great Expedition, the honor and the hopes. He remembered the reception at Joseph Delisle's and thought it had been given in honor of the Commander and that he had been present. His mind ran on back, to an evening seventeen years before. He remembered the imposing stranger who strode across the crowded hall to speak with the czar on his deathbed. So much honor and envy! To come from that to this lonely island, this slate-gray face and louse-infested body—surely that was a terrible thing!

Steller knew that this was a terrible thing and was frightened because for a moment he could not feel its awfulness. The dead man at his feet silently denied it; the cold, eternal rocks before him and the deep roar of the sea at his back echoed indifference to such codes. For a moment Steller heard the voice of the wilderness and trembled before awful doubt. But the men were waiting for him. He began to speak at random.

"Vitus Bering was a Dane by birth, a righteous and devout Christian, a man of good manners, kind, quiet, and universally liked by the whole command, both high and low. Fair-minded persons cannot but admit that to the best of his strength and ability he tried at all times to carry out the task imposed upon him.

"He perished from hunger, cold, thirst, lice, and grief rather than from any disease and would undoubtedly have stayed alive if he had reached Kamchatka. A warm bed and fresh food were all he needed.

"His calmness and earnest preparation for the parting were admirable. He was concerned only for the welfare of his command, without care for his own life, and had no more heartfelt wish than our deliverance from this country and his own deliverance from misery. . . ."

Kind, quiet, and universally liked. Was Steller speaking of the Commander or of Betge? He saw very little difference between these men and would have used the same words for Betge. But they would not have been true. Steller, who was neither kind nor quiet, and who had no wish to be liked, did not know the meaning of the words he used. He was lamely saying what little good he could find to say about a man he did not respect. He did not know that these pale virtues characterize the strong man. He had not heard the warning of the prophet that the truly great man "hath no form nor comeliness, and when we shall see him there is no beauty that we should desire him."

Steller had finished. He stopped thinking. And then the naked truth which pressed on him from all sides spoke through him.

"He could not have found a better place to prepare for Eternity than this deathbed under the open sky."

Sickness and fatigue in the men around him, death itself in the motionless body of the Commander, and the cold, bleak world in which they stood were alike indifferent to Steller's words. No one heard what he said. The men swayed on their feet, aware only that the Commander was having a proper burial. Betge sat on the sand, rocking his body in anguish. A warm bed was all he needed! A warm bed. Steller could have given him that. But he made soup for Mr. Plenisner instead.

When they returned to the pit for the belated breakfast Steller was silent and obviously troubled about something. But he was not thinking of Vitus Bering or of the wilderness. By the time they sat down to eat he had made up his mind.

"Did you notice Lieutenant Waxel?" he asked. "He is a very sick man."

The others nodded and stirred their soup. This seemed a dull and obvious fact that led nowhere.

"He does not have Master Khitrov's extraordinary physique," Steller went on. "And I very much doubt if he can pull through without some help. On his death the command would fall to Khitrov. I believe, in such a case, the universal hatred for this man would destroy all discipline and perhaps prevent our deliverance. Seeing that the welfare of all is at stake, I think we should forget our grievances against the lieutenant and arrange some sort of shelter for him where he can rest. Our cossacks could dig such a pit very quickly. . . ."

Roselius had listened, not daring to let his mind run ahead, until Steller himself had said the words. He now tried to conceal his pleasure.

"Yes. You are quite right. He is so badly ravaged by this scurvy, I had given him up for lost. But a place to himself would make a difference. It might be all he needed."

Betge joined in. "That would be very good! Very good of you, Dr. Steller. Very humane—considering all we have had to suffer from this man."

Steller called the two servants of the dead Commander and put them to work with his own men, promising them that from now on they would work for him and be cared for by him. Roselius, Betge, and Plenisner joined the men and in a short time the pit was dug. Under Roselius' orders they lined and roofed it with wood and then fastened down the sail covering. When it was finished and a fire had been lighted at the entrance Roselius and Betge went into the barracks to find Waxel.

He lay on the ground, exhausted by the exertion of the morning, unconscious of the horrors around him, but tossing and moaning to their noise. His servant was sleeping beside him. Roselius wakened the man. Then he lifted the unconscious officer by the shoulders, while Betge took his knees. Swaying and stumbling, they made their way along the trench and out across the sands.

The clumsy movements and the jolting brought Waxel to painful consciousness without his having sufficient strength to understand what was being done to him. Then he was put down in strange, restful silence. He opened his eyes and saw the ceiling boards over his head. His eyes ran over the walls and floor. He understood. He was being given a place to himself, because he would die without it. He remembered Khitrov. He remembered that the Commander was dead and he, Waxel, was in command. His eyes ran over the faces of the men standing around him. The soldier Plenisner was smiling stupidly. Steller was talking about something, explaining something. Betge was looking at him, dumb and unhappy. There was Roselius looking at him too, with a stony, expressionless face. Then his eyes fell on his own servant. He motioned, and the man stepped forward and bent over to hear what was said.

"Khitrov! Bring Khitrov here!" he said clearly.

He saw that everyone had heard and understood, and sank into unconsciousness again.

By January Steller had his house in perfect order. Roselius supplied the meat, Betge the driftwood for fuel. Steller was in charge of the cooking and all indoor concerns. Plenisner varied his services between hunting and getting wood. The five servants now slept in an adjoining pit but they worked under Steller's direction, assisting him or being sent by him to help Roselius or Betge.

Pleased with the order he had created and anxious to display it, Steller sent Thomas across the snow to invite the officers to tea the following Sunday. After two months of cold, nakedness, hunger, and disease, this echo of civilized life caused considerable excitement and even nervousness. Waxel and Khitrov spent the next few days talking about the coming tea party. Before leaving their pit on Sunday afternoon they tried to pull their makeshift clothes into some kind of order.

"Remember," Waxel told Khitrov, "you're not to quarrel with him. You're not to contradict anything he says. We agree with him all the time."

"I won't forget. No matter what he says, it's 'Yes sir! That's right! That's quite right!' "

Steller received his guests cordially. He took them by the hand and led them around the fire to the interior of the pit where bedding had been piled for seats. Roselius and Betge nodded to the officers without speaking. The hosts all seemed a little nervous except Plenisner, who was cutting shoes from a provision sack and did not stop his work. When they were seated Steller passed the tea and then lifted his cup.

"To Her Majesty!"

The six men, squatting against the walls in the small, dark pit, drank the toast in tea. Waxel thought, "Her Majesty! It's three years since we've had news from Moscow. Her Majesty may be dead for all we know." Thinking simply of dead rulers, he responded with the second toast.

"To the great Czar Peter." All eyes turned on him in surprise, and he rounded out the words with an explanation.

"We have come to this place through his will; may his spirit take us home."

Steller was pleased that his party was going so well. He said happily, "Really, we can feel as much enjoyment in this shadowy place as in other places where everything is in abundance!"

"That is right!" said Khitrov.

Steller felt the unnatural tone in his voice. "We have a great deal of comfort here as a matter of fact. Many people living in proper homes are not as well off as we are."

"That is right!" Khitrov repeated.

Steller was annoyed. "I wish I could say as much for the barracks! There day and night is spent in wretched gambling with cards. Nothing is talked of but card playing. This must certainly be a source of hate and quarreling among them. I think as shipmaster it is your duty to put a stop to it. If this passion gets the upper hand of the men you will never restore discipline."

Khitrov put his face down close to his cup and said, "It wouldn't be right for me to stop it, Mr. Steller. You see, I've won nearly everything they've got."

"We're living under extraordinary conditions," Waxel said, anxious to keep the peace. "I think some laxness is in place. If we should meet some great misfortune later on, the friendship of these men would mean more than authority."

Steller felt his position as host and he too tried to be friendly. "We are indeed living under extraordinary circumstances. Precious furs no longer have any value and are left lying around to be chewed to pieces by foxes. On the other hand, axes, knives, shoes, strings, and such objects have become precious. Rank, learning, and other distinctions are of no advantage here. Where no one will work for money, we must each be shoemaker, butcher, footman as best we can. Hereafter we could probably all of us earn a good living in any of these trades!" He laughed at his joke and then went on seriously, "I do think we have organized this household very well. Everyone here knows his duty and his business without having to be reminded of it. We manage our cossacks in such a way——"

"One of your Cossacks is a Finn and the rest are Kamchatkans," Khitrov interrupted.

Steller stopped for a minute to consider what Khitrov had said. He did not hear it as a contradiction, but as a statement of fact about his cossacks. He went on, "We manage them in such a way that they are at our service at all times and obey us in all matters. In return they receive their household goods from us. We have the advantage that we Germans do not have to build fires, fetch water, nor open or close the chimney. After meals the kitchen and table utensils are rinsed and put away by them and everything is done in an orderly manner."

Plenisner went on with his sewing. Neither Waxel nor Khitrov had heard anything surprising in Steller's speech. But Betge and Roselius looked at each other in amazement. The question which had troubled both of them for two months had been answered. We Germans.

Betge shriveled even further, terrified to think that his health, perhaps his life, had turned on something so beyond a man's control. The effect on Roselius was quite different. "Nothing I do will alter that!" he thought, and laughed. Then he turned to Khitrov and spoke for the first time that afternoon.

"As soon as we get the spring thaw, I will go to Avacha for help."

The words rang with defiance in that shelter, built in the faith that this was a desert island. But Steller was unruffled.

"You will not reach Avacha, but I suppose someone will have to try," he said.

15. THE "ST. PETER" RETURNS

TOWARD the end of March there was promise of spring. The snow melted along the beaches and driftwood came into sight. A number of expeditions set out for Avacha, but they quickly turned into hunting parties. After a few days the men would return to camp with food but no information about the land they were on.

This hunting was strenuous work. Each man carried an ax and leather working tools. By this time the leather provision sacks had been cut up into shoes and these too had worn out. Any tear in leather had to be mended the minute it occurred. A find of food or wood was carried back to camp on a yoke.

The otter had practically disappeared, but the fur seal, or sea bear as these men called it, was beginning to come ashore on the west side of the island. These were the bulls, which came ahead of the herd. They fought each other savagely, staining the sands with red blood, and their bellowing could be heard in camp. Their meat was particularly repulsive, even to Steller, and produced vomiting and diarrhea in the men. Khitrov says the flesh "was quite distasteful and the longer we ate it the less we liked it."

Solitary sea lions also came ashore. But the men were afraid to attack this animal, even in a body. This was Steller's Sea Lion—the most ferocious beast of the sea, hooded with long fur which resembled a lion's mane, as unlike the familiar sea lion as his sea cow was the manatee.

The third week in April, Alexei Ivanov actually traveled two hundred miles and returned to camp with the news that they were on an island. This probably surprised no one. But it put an end to such expeditions. From that time on they knew that they would have to build a boat to get away in.

To break up the *St. Peter* and build another ship was to destroy government property without orders, and so called for divided responsibility. The day after Ivanov returned Waxel called the men together around the wrecked hull and asked their opinion about its seaworthiness. The bottom, keel, sternpost, and stem were all damaged; the rudder was lost; there were no anchors; the ship was so deeply buried in the sand that it could not be moved—therefore it was not fit for further service. A paper stating these facts had been prepared and was passed among the men for their signatures. Ovtsin refused to sign.

"We can't stay here on that account," Waxel said. "You can write a counterstatement and I'll send it in."

Ovtsin drew up a counterstatement. "The sternpost and stem are not so badly injured that they cannot be repaired; the false stem is gone, but another can be made; another rudder can be made; we have not yet tried to recover the anchors. At present it is difficult to say how badly damaged the bottom is, and even if it were, it could be repaired. It is difficult to say whether the ship can be moved. These are my views and these are the reasons why I refuse to sign the report to the effect that the ship is unfit for further service."

Ovtsin felt that his objections proved he was a better officer than Waxel. Waxel read the report and was no longer afraid of Ovtsin. He had shown that he protested merely for the sake of protesting. What he might say about the landing did not matter now.

The true spring came suddenly, in May. The snows thawed almost overnight, rain fell steadily for a week, and the streams overflowed. Water rose in the pits. The men were driven

above ground and made themselves tents of sailcloth. When
the rains stopped the world had changed. Small quantities of
grass appeared, out of which the Kamchatkans made wine.
The sea cows were making love, the female "fleeing slowly
before the male with continual turns about." The foxes had
lost their hair, and with only wool on them looked as if they
were in their underclothes. They were accompanied by large
litters and barked savagely at the men, ordering them away
from their young.

The rains were followed by fog. Through the winter
months the wind had blown continually; the men had become
accustomed to its howl and to staggering against it on their
difficult journeys across the island. Now it suddenly dropped,
the roar of the sea sounded in their ears again, and the fog
closed around them. Under cover of the fog, the seal herds
came ashore.

Building a ship was a great deal of labor, and the work of
breaking up the *St. Peter* went ahead listlessly. Supplies were
dug out of the hull and placed on the beach. There were
grindstones to be dressed and tools to be cleaned and sharp-
ened. The carpenter refused to break up the ship without the
proper tools. Crowbars, wedges, and hammers had to be
forged. For this it was necessary to gather wood to make
charcoal, and none of the men wanted to look for driftwood.

A kind of community life was organized to facilitate the
work. The men were divided into relays for carpentering,
hunting, and cooking. But all the men went hunting, even
when they were supposed to be cooking or building. At one
time the carpenter, the only man among them who knew how
to construct a ship, was away for two weeks and everyone
supposed he had been killed.

Four weeks after the decision to break up the *St. Peter*,
nothing had been done. But Waxel, hoping to give the men
an impetus to work, announced that building on the new

vessel would begin. Posts were to be set up on the beach thirty-six feet apart to mark the keel, and they would all drink to their prosperity in saturan.

The morning was spent making saturan. The ill-tasting flour was roasted brown, then mixed to a paste in seal oil and thinned out with hot water. It was drunk hot like tea. Waxel's ceremony pleased the men. They enjoyed the saturan; they enjoyed the toasting; their spirits rose with the thought of going home. The posts were duly set up. But the enthusiasm did not last overnight, and the next day no more work than usual was done.

Many things occurred to raise the spirits of the men. One morning the carpenter was shouting so excitedly that all came out of their tents to see. He was dragging a plank and calling to everyone to look at it, to look at the ax marks on it. They were his own cuts; this was lumber he had worked on in Avacha! The men looked with awe at this piece of wood which had come to them from home, and Waxel set it up on the beach as an omen of good luck.

Another day, men who had been sent to the far side of the island to gather wood came running into camp without wood and very excited. Standing on the western shore and looking out across the water, they had seen, unmistakable, white against blue, the snow-capped mountains of Kamchatka! Spirits rose. The camp seethed with excitement. But the work did not go ahead.

As the spring rains drove the men above ground, Steller's worst fears were realized—the passion for gambling had indeed got the upper hand. The surer the men felt of returning to Kamchatka, the more important their winnings became. Each encouraging fact, which Waxel hoped would set them to work, merely raised the price of fur and sent the men back to their cards with new enthusiasm. Ten weeks passed after they began to break up the *St. Peter* and nothing was done.

Waxel explains the delay as being due to "the great distance from the source of authority," and Khitrov says the same thing in plainer words: "The men were in such poor condition and so undisciplined that it was not safe to order them around." The authority which might have moved these men was not in St. Petersburg, and it was merely formal courtesy on Waxel's part to speak as if it were. It had rested in the body of the Commander, which now lay beneath the sand. But perhaps the men had sunk to a point at which even the Commander could not have moved them. In any case, at the beginning of July there was no reason to suppose that these men would ever leave the island.

Steller spent a great deal of time watching the sea cow, sketching it, speculating about it, and wishing that one would die and be washed ashore so that he could dissect it. Shoeless men, setting out on the long, cross-country search for food, looked covetously at the "cabbage eater"—tons of placid flesh browsing quietly along the beaches. But this was not the sort of thing one can draw out with a hook. Several times during June parties of men climbed over the rocks with grappling hooks hoping to haul one of these animals ashore. But the hide of the sea cow was unbelievably tough. The hooks did not penetrate, but slid over the animals as if they were granite boulders.

Steller watched several of these unsuccessful attempts before the answer occurred to him. That day the blacksmith was throwing the hook. Again and again it struck an animal, only to slide down its back into the water.

"I still say it's food," the blacksmith was saying as Steller came up.

"You can hardly expect to take an animal of this size without a harpoon," Steller said.

"A harpoon!" the blacksmith exclaimed. "Of course that's what we want! A harpoon!"

In a few minutes everyone knew that the smith was going to get a cabbage eater. They gathered around the forge, telling how it should be done. None of these men had ever been whaling, but everyone knew someone who had. Between them they worked out a strategy for hunting the sea cow. The harpoon was to have two lines. One was to be carried in the longboat by six men, with the smith in charge as harpooner. The other line was to be held on shore by forty men who would follow the boat along the beach and be ready to pull when the battle began.

Fortunately it was not a whale they were hunting, but one of the most helpless animals that ever lived. The sea cow could do nothing but eat. It had no fangs or claws. It could not lash its enormous tail of solid fat. With only two short feet, it could not even kick.

The next morning everyone was ready. The longboat rowed into a river mouth, badly hampered by the shore line, which caught on projecting rocks and had to be untangled again and again. In spite of this the boat was able to move well into the herd. When they had worked their way close to the shore, the harpoon was thrown and sank deep into the flesh of a cow. The struck cow lifted its head and snorted, rolling slightly from side to side. A shout went up on shore and the forty men began to pull. The six men in the boat used their line to drag themselves close to the animal. When the boat ground along its back the men were ready with axes and knives and began to hack at it, hoping to "weary" it. They soon found that the abdomen, which protruded widely on both sides, was vulnerable. At any break in the skin there, the intestines would bulge through with a loud whistling noise. In a few minutes the herd was in great confusion. With no comprehension of an attack, with no fear for themselves, they understood that their gasping companion was in trouble and that this trouble was drawing her to land. They tried to get between the wounded animal and the shore. Jostling and pushing, they threw their weight against the strength of the forty men. But the tide was ebbing, and as the water moved out the animals were forced to go with it, leaving the cow which could not follow. By the time the tide returned the men had drawn the carcass safely up on the beach. A bull came partly out of the water, peered at his companion and snorted as if to ask her how she was, and then joined the others at their incessant grazing.

Everyone was excited. The animal was thirty-five feet long and weighed approximately twenty tons. Slices of dark red flesh which looked like meat that had been preserved in salt-peter were cut out and put on to boil. In boiling they swelled to twice their size and were thoroughly cooked in half an hour. It tasted like the finest veal. In the meantime some of the fat had been tried out. It tasted like sweet almond oil, and the men drank it by the cupful without being nauseated. One easy killing had brought more than three tons of fine-tasting food.

The flesh of an animal which lived on seaweed might be expected to have peculiar properties, and there were two surprising things about the meat of the sea cow. In the first place, it did not spoil easily. It was stored on high platforms, out of reach of the foxes, lying in the open sun for weeks. Blowflies swarmed about it and covered it with worms. But it never became rancid; it never lost its fine fresh flavor. In the second place, it proved an instantaneous cure for scurvy. Bering's men had come on this island almost dead from a lack of fresh food. Since then their only food had been fish-eating animals. They were still very close to death, but they had grown accustomed to it and did not know it. They needed green plants, or at least the meat of grass-eating animals. And apparently seaweed

was more potent than land grass. Two days after the sea cow
had been killed, a change came over the camp. Everyone became cheerful and energetic. Each man remembered what
health was like, and realized that until that moment he had
been very sick!

The gambling stopped; everywhere men were working enthusiastically. The old hull dissolved and a new one rose beside
it. Men willingly brought wood from any distance, and the
forge blazed continually. Some men were trying out tar from
old ropes; others were mending sails; others had erected an
oven and were baking biscuit for the voyage from the flour
remaining from the *St. Peter*. Water casks were overhauled,
bound with new hoops, and filled. The longboat went out
each afternoon, dragging the bay for anchors. In five weeks
the hooker was ready for the sea.

The hooker was named *St. Peter* and launched with due
ceremony on August seventeenth. After public prayers for a
safe voyage the forty-six men lifted the ropes to slide her down
the ways. As the ship moved to their pull, the men remembered the world they were returning to and began to sing.

> *Now, my boys, we'll pull together,*
> *Pull the pole with all our strength.*
> *Ho! the pole, the towing pole,*
> *Ho! the green one, she moves alone.*
> *She moves, she moves, she moves.*

The *St. Peter* moved on for fifteen or twenty feet and then
stopped. The makeshift ways, built of driftwood held in place
by cannon, had sunk under her weight. The men ran for
planks and jacks and soon got her off the sand. But meanwhile
the tide had ebbed, and it was the next day before the *St.
Peter* was actually floated. Under better circumstances this
would have been an ill omen indeed, but on the shores of

Commander Island it was only a slight hardship in the miracle of getting a ship afloat.

The hooker lay in the bay for six days. During that time masts were set, shrouds made fast, water and baggage brought on board. For provisions there were great quantities of sea-cow meat. Each member of the crew was allowed personal baggage, varying from seventy to seven hundred pounds, according to rank.

There were goods remaining from the old ship—cannon and cannon balls, casks and pieces of sail—which were not taken on the hooker. They were safely stored away in a shelter built for that purpose. But Khitrov was uneasy about them. He drew up a statement as to why it had been necessary to leave them and had every man in the company sign it.

To take all the material along would oblige us to leave behind half or more of the crew, and to leave these men on an unknown and uninhabited island is dangerous. There is little food to be had here aside from what may be obtained by hunting sea animals, and even this source cannot be depended upon.

Although a small part of the above-mentioned material is good, yet it is not worth while to leave someone to watch it, because the island is uninhabited. If we should leave a guard, we would have to come after him next year. There is no harbor here, nothing but rocks and reefs and the open sea, and there is great danger of wrecking the vessel.

Khitrov's worry over these goods seems excessive, if the hooker actually could not carry them. The baggage of the crew came to more than three tons, and Khitrov's record does not show what personal property these shipwrecked sailors had, for which he was abandoning good government cannon balls. But Steller says that the *St. Peter* took back with her more than nine hundred otter skins.

On the afternoon of August twenty-third the men were ready to go on board. But first they walked back across the dunes to the place where they had buried the Commander eight months before. Waxel put up a wooden cross.

"We place this monument as a memorial to the Captain Commander and as a sign of our having taken possession of this land for the Russian Empire.'"

The next morning, warping with the anchor, the *St. Peter* moved out beyond the reef and set her course for Kamchatka. The fog was settling in a fine rain. On shore the foxes swarmed over the abandoned camp, finding themselves suddenly unmolested by man and in possession of enormous quantities of meat and fat.

Returning to the sea, to life as it had always been, the men were filled with strange regrets. Every mountain and valley on this barren rock was familiar to them and saturate with memories. They stood at the rail, discussing the price of fur and arguing whether it would not have been worth while to spend another winter there and truly make their fortunes out of pelts. Steller was shocked by such avarice, but he too watched the island slip by with nostalgia. Then he saw Khitrov standing near him. The master was looking sadly at the shore.

"I am sorry that no ice formed in the rivers this winter," Steller said. "I would have liked to confirm a theory of mine, that ice drifts from here to the mainland."

The *St. Peter* was badly overloaded. The men slept in the hold, which was filled with supplies and baggage to within three feet of the deck. The crew was divided into three watches, and two sleeping places given to three men. But even two thirds of the crew could not crawl into the hold at the same time.

A few hours after they lost sight of the island the *St. Peter* sprung a leak. Baggage was hauled on deck as fast as possible, and as much government property as had been taken along was thrown over. The water rose rapidly and the pumps would not work. The men had forgotten to put strainers on them and they had clogged with chips left in the hold. Through the night the whole crew was in the water, bailing with buckets and cooking pans. The carpenter would not lend a hand. He stood with water slopping around his knees, too dumfounded to care whether they sank or not.

"I did not build a leaky boat!" he announced at intervals.

After a few hours this confidence bore fruit. The carpenter suddenly remembered the collapse on the ways, and the jacks. He remembered which jack had been misplaced and which plank it had loosened. His memory was so exact that he was able to mend the leak under three feet of water. The next day they put strainers on the pumps and returned the baggage to the hold.

The following day they reached Kamchatka. They were only three miles from shore when they saw the land looming through the mist. The *St. Peter* moved back out to sea and followed the coast down to Avacha. This journey of about a hundred miles took ten days. The winds either did not blow at all or were against them, and most of the distance was made by rowing. The night of September fifth was clear, with stars shining. They rowed through the night, making a mile every three hours. In the early morning they passed the Vauna lighthouse which they themselves had built, and at dawn were in Avacha Bay.

A Kamchatkan skin boat was coming out of the harbor. When it had come within shouting distance of the ship one of the men stood up and called to them, asking who they were. Waxel answered:

"The *St. Peter*. Returning from America."

The little boat quickly came alongside. Checking his real

question, "How many of you are still alive?", the leader asked, "Who is in command?"

"I am. Lieutenant Waxel."

For a few minutes no one found anything to say. The *St. Peter's* men had forgotten what things they wanted to know, what things men asked each other, and the men in the small boat were embarrassed.

"The *St. Paul* came in last year," someone said at last.

Then everyone began to talk. The story of the *St. Paul* was told. But the *St. Peter's* men were not interested. They could tell more than that.

"All the officers had died except Captain Chirikov, and he was dying."

"Where is Captain Chirikov now?" Waxel asked.

But the men did not know. "He has left. Everybody has left."

Finally the leader of the small boat touched the delicate point. "We thought the *St. Peter* was lost," he said. "The things you left here have been carried off by various people."

"The storehouse has been rifled?" Waxel shouted.

His words were drowned in the clamor that rose from the *St. Peter*. Each man had lost something precious. They shouted at the men in the small boat, cursing and threatening, or, exhausted by their anger, sank down on the deck moaning their loss. The men in the small boat stared at the ship in terror and fascination. They tried to soften the story—there were a few things left here and there; they had seen a sack; perhaps some of the things could be found.

Surprised by the noise that rose around him, surprised by his own anger, Waxel looked from the men in the small boat to the men on the *St. Peter*. He saw the terror in the traders' eyes and he saw his shipmates through those eyes—men in sailcloth smocks, barelegged, bare-armed, their faces covered with beards, their long hair hanging to their shoulders. He saw a sailor lying on the deck, shaken with sobs. The man had just gained his life. But what of that? He had lost a pair of shoes. Understanding the traders and understanding the sailor, Waxel began to laugh. He lifted his hand to his own beard and laughed harder. He had told these men that this savage was Lieutenant Waxel! He had told them that this hooker was the *St. Peter*. Waxel's laugh, ringing out over the cries of the men, was the last touch of horror for the sober men in the small boat. They pushed off from the ship and rowed for the harbor as fast as they could.

Waxel, still laughing, staggered to the hatch to go below. He was suddenly very sleepy. Khitrov looked at him in alarm.

"What are the orders? Shall we row in?" he asked.

"Row if you like. If you don't someone will tow you."

Such orders frightened Khitrov. He called for the oars. And the *St. Peter* began its long, three-hour drag across the bay.

THE SHAKEN MISTS

---

16. MAKING THE MAP

THE HARBOR of the Holy Apostles, abandoned by the crews, had been taken over by the traders from the Upper Post. Perhaps the fury of the *St. Peter's* men when they heard that their personal property had been stolen was largely shock at the fact that they had been looked on as dead. If so, a worse shock awaited them. On shore they found men who had never heard of them and who had to be told who they were. But the traders received the sailors cordially. Waxel was given Bering's cabin, and all treated as honored guests.

Waxel remained at St. Peter and St. Paul for a year. He walked alone by the sea or sat in the hall with the men, listening to their stories with amused indifference. He had a report to make, but was in no hurry to make it or to do anything else.

"Nobody's waiting for this," he explained. "They believe we're dead and they can believe that for another winter."

Khitrov watched him anxiously, conscious that this was not

the same man he had lived with on the island. Such laxness was out of place in an officer. But what disturbed Khitrov most was Waxel's laugh. It was not a small laugh, at something a man could see; it ran under everything, found everything funny.

"It is unsettling," Khitrov decided.

Waxel was thinking of his report. "I am recommending Ovtsin for reinstatement," he said.

Khitrov stared at him.

"You wouldn't want him serving under you on another voyage, would you?" Waxel asked, and laughed.

"Two officers are returning from this expedition," Khitrov said slowly. "One of them is dying. The other is mad."

"I am not mad, Master Khitrov," Waxel answered seriously. "Madmen are unhappy. And I will enjoy anything that happens to me, as long as I live."

The members of the crew, steaming in the bathhouse, warmed by fires that did not smoke, unmolested by foxes, ate good red meat and drank good vodka. The life they had just escaped from—which had been merely life as they lived through it—now seemed unreal, incredible, and ludicrous. As shipwrecked mariners it was their privilege to tell tales of amazing hardship, and they began to talk. But their story took its shape from their audience, men in fur-lined coats and hoods leaning against the cabin walls, Siberian fur traders, too familiar with hardship to be interested in hearing about more.

"Blue foxes?" they asked incredulously, hungrily.

"Yes. Blue. And thick as lice."

"Sea otters?"

"The otters come ashore to get killed." The men laid out their furs.

"The sea bear?"

"The sea bear breeds there."

These men who had sailed out of port on a wild-goose

chase, searching for the fairyland of Juan de Gama, with its gold and its pearls, had returned with a tale too fantastic for Juan de Gama to have dreamed of.

"Two days' sail from the mouth of the Kamchatka!"

During that winter all the traders on Kamchatka heard the story and came into St. Peter and St. Paul to hear it again. They listened with staring eyes and clenched fists. They studied the chart from the *St. Peter* and made copies of it. The next spring a hundred boats would find those rocks lying in the smoky sea—and the islands beyond—and the islands beyond—until the traders had reached the mainland of America.

At St. Peter and St. Paul the traders had not been interested in the wonders of the sea cow. But the *St. Peter's* men insisted on telling about it.

"It's *the* cure for scurvy. I had scurvy for ten months and this cured me in a day!"

"This meat never spoils. You can see for yourself."

"The doctors in St. Petersburg ought to know about this," the traders said kindly, but without interest.

But as they began to make the long journey to America, the traders remembered this meat. The sea cow was easy to kill, easy to pack, and its anti-scurvy powers proved to be remarkable. Soon no boat left Kamchatka for the east without stopping for a load of sea-cow meat. Each summer the ships put into that bay. The traders saw the lonely cross that marked the grave of the great Commander. Filling their ships with food for the long voyage, they turned to that grave for God-speed. Without leave of the cartographers, the island became Commander's Island, and the seas beyond, Bering's Sea.

The history of the North Pacific passed into the hands of the traders; the Senate and the Academy faded to dim voices four thousand miles away. When the reports from the *St. Peter* reached Moscow they were considered carefully. The Senate

considered them and the Academy of Science considered
them. Eventually new men were sent to check on the facts.
But by the time these men reached the Pacific the traders had
their posts in America, the cross that marked the grave was
gone, and the last sea cow in the world had been eaten. On
Commander Island there were only dry bones to verify
Steller's accounts.

The work had been done. The way was known, and men
were swarming over the steppingstones to America. But the
problems of exploration had been foregotten in Moscow.
When the first news from the *St. Peter* reached there, late in
1743, the expedition which had left eleven years before was
remembered vaguely and the *Gazette de France* covered the
whole matter with an obscure notice of loss at sea.

*Captain Behring, who went to discover whether one could
go to America by way of the North Pacific, wrecked and lost
his boat on the coast of a desert island on which he and the
greater part of his crew that accompanied him died.*

Three years later George Steller died, on his way back from
Siberia. This concerned the Academy, and the announcement
of Steller's death was worded after his own heart.

*Mr. George William Steller of Windsheim, Franconia, fa-
mous botanist and professor of the Imperial Academy, died
recently between Tobolsk and Catherinesburg. The loss of
this scholar is generally regretted. He was on his way from
Kamchatka after having discovered one of the islands of North
America and proved that it was only a short distance thither
from the Russian Empire. He undertook this voyage of discovery by order of the Court with Captain Bering in command
of the ship. They had the misfortune to be wrecked on an
unknown island where the captain and a large number of*

*those who were on board died of misery and grief. Mr. Steller,
with the help of seven others who survived, made a small
boat from the remains of the wreck and returned to Kamchatka. Among his papers are a number of very valuable
reports which at the request of the deceased were forwarded
to the Academy, and there is reason to believe that these documents will soon be made public.*

George Steller had left St. Peter and St. Paul as soon as he
landed there. He could not endure another day in the company of the men with whom he had spent fifteen months.
Taking Plenisner with him, he crossed Kamchatka on foot
and spent the winter on the western shore. Here he worked
on his book, *De bestiis marinis*. He also wrote letters to his
friends in Moscow, familiar, chatty letters, damning to everyone who had sailed on the *St. Peter*, and Steller's version of the
voyage became tradition. He promised to send his friends
an account of his scientific observations as soon as he could
get them copied, but could not say how soon that would be.

"Mr. Plenisner is a great thief of time," he explained. It is
pleasant to think that Steller found something worth neglect-
ing his duty for.

The next summer, instead of going to Okhotsk and on
toward civilization, Steller bought a boat and returned to
Commander Island. He spent a full year there. In the fall of
1744 he had reached Yakutsk, but even then did not go direct
to Russia. He made short expeditions to various parts of
Siberia. All of these involved hardship and were done in the
interest of science. But perhaps Steller had been happier in
the wilderness than he ever was in Moscow.

In the fall of 1746 he had reached Tobolsk—civilization,
roads, transportation, and taverns—the road home. A day's
journey into Russia, he stopped at a tavern to eat and drink,
while his man waited with the sleigh in the falling snow. Stel-

ler left the tavern very drunk. He stumbled onto the floor of
his sleigh and lay there in a stupor. The man, seeing that the
master would not be conscious for some time, went inside himself and drank till dawn. And George Steller, lying on the rugs
that should have covered him, was frozen to death.

On an evening in 1747 Joseph Delisle's sleigh waited at the
gate of Captain Alexei Chirikov, and the old man stood by the
bed looking sadly at the sunken cheeks and frail hands of the
captain.

Chirikov had been carried from the *St. Paul* very near death
from scurvy and tuberculosis, and he never recovered. After
reaching Moscow he saw few people, but the old astronomer
was hard to refuse.

"The scurvy sleeps in my system and I cannot shake it off,"
Chirikov was saying.

Delisle lowered his eyes. He knew that scurvy did not
linger, and he supposed the captain knew this too. He drew
up a chair and took a roll of paper from his coat.

"This is an account of your voyage to America. I am anxious to read it to you, to make sure there is no mistake."

Chirikov nodded for him to go ahead, and the old man
began to read. "The voyage from Kamchatka to America
made by Captain Alexis Chirikov and my brother. Captain
Alexis Chirikov, with my brother on board, departed June
15, 1741, from the port of St. Peter and St. Paul——"

Chirikov's mind slipped from the reading. To him the
Great Expedition to America was a bottomless horror of loss.
His Russian lieutenants lay in the sea; Delisle, the Frenchman,
in the port on Kamchatka; Bering, the Dane, on a nameless
island; Steller, the German, in the mountains of Siberia. Chirikov knew that he would not correct anything Joseph Delisle
found to say. He watched the old man turning his papers.
Should he tell him that his brother Louis knew nothing about

astronomy, that all his figures were meaningless? He would not do that. What if Joseph Delisle formed wrong opinions about the coast of America? What if the French Academy was misled? What did such things matter, compared with hurting an old man?

"On the return voyage my brother fell ill, October 8, 1741, and died October twentieth at ten o'clock in the morning."

Joseph Delisle had finished. Chirikov looked at him in surprise.

"He has left us out at sea. He might have brought us into port," he thought. But as he watched Joseph, who sat stooped over his papers staring before him with unseeing eyes, Chirikov changed his mind. "No. Louis is dead. The story is finished."

This brother whom Joseph was mourning was not an astronomer; he knew nothing about measurements, and cared nothing. But he had known life; and he had still been able to laugh and sing.

"Your brother was a very great man," Chirikov said with sudden, heartfelt sincerity.

Tears welled in Joseph Delisle's eyes and he took out his handkerchief. "Unless I make something from his figures, that will never be known," he said. Then he stood up. "I am afraid I have wearied you."

"No. I am glad you came. And I could not say that of any other man in Moscow."

"Then I am glad I came. By next spring you will be too strong to welcome the company of an old man," and Joseph smiled gallantly.

Joseph Delisle's study was more subdued than it had been fifteen years before. He burned fewer candles because he felt that the light tired his old eyes. But there was the same rich comfort, the same shimmer of heavy silks. Brocaded draperies covered the windows and hid the falling snow.

Joseph opened his desk and placed the paper which he had just read to Captain Chirikov with another which he hoped to read to him some time: "Report on the inhabitants found in a port near Kamchatka by Captain Alexis Chirikov and my brother in the voyage which they made to America." He then took out his scrapbook. He hesitated to start any serious work because he was expecting a visit from General Pissarjev that evening.

This gentleman, who had been exiled to Siberia for political reasons, had recently been pardoned and restored to rank. He had been in Eastern Siberia at the time the Kamchatka Expedition was there, and had known everyone. He talked a great deal about Louis Delisle. Joseph knew very well that the general's mind wandered, that he confused Louis with other people, but it was pleasant to hear him talk. And Joseph believed that he was able to glean some true facts from the general's hazy reminiscing.

Opening his scrapbook, Joseph took up the announcement of George Steller's death which he had torn from a paper a few weeks before and trimmed it neatly. As he pasted it under the notice of the wreck of the *St. Peter* his tears dropped on the page. The terrible price that is paid for knowledge! Leaving the desk, he went over to his map of the North Pacific which hung on the wall.

This was the map which would go to the French Academy as the result of Bering's voyages. Joseph believed that it was based on his brother Louis's figures. But it was based more on Joseph's own passion for compromise. Nothing that Joseph had ever heard about the North Pacific had been discarded and nothing had been taken at its face value. The beautiful chart from the *St. Peter*, which showed the line of the Aleutian chain so clearly, had been sacrificed to make room for the lands of Juan de Gama and Bartholomew de Fonte. All that remained of it was a small island near Kamchatka, called Bering-land. The mainland of America, which had been reached by Chirikov, was shown as a large island, Chirikovland.

This was the chart which Peter had asked Bering to send. But only the houses of Delisle speak to the Academies of Science, and Bering's chart had already gone to the traders of Siberia.

The tears still running over his face, Joseph Delisle took up his charcoal and made the island discovered by Vitus Bering a little larger than it had been. That seemed the least he could do, in the face of so much suffering.

A servant announced General Pissarjev. The old man, cared for by servants and wearing the insignia of his rank, now rode through the city which had once feared him, and saw no one who remembered his name. It was no longer himself, but his world, that had died, and he was content. But in all Moscow there was no one with whom he could spend an evening except the astronomer Delisle. And Delisle welcomed him because he was interested in Kamchatka! This seemed an irony to Pissarjev. He would have liked it better if the scholar had been interested in Peter. But he knew what was owing to a host and talked about Kamchatka constantly.

Joseph led him to a comfortable chair, facing the map, and then pointed out the changes he had just made in it.

"Yes. I think you are right. I remember now, it was a good-sized island," Pissarjev said.

Joseph was annoyed. "You don't remember, General Pissarjev! This island was not known when you were in Siberia."

But Joseph's anger could not last. He too needed someone to talk to. He brought out a brandy and poured a glass for each of them.

"I have drawn my map chiefly from observations made by my brother while he was aboard the *St. Paul*," Joseph said, lifting his glass.

"Your brother was a wonderful man." Pissarjev choked on

his brandy. His face turned a dark red and the scar showed white. He drew out a handkerchief to wipe his eyes.

The scent which the general was using was too heavy for Joseph Delisle's taste, and he moved away hurriedly. To cover his retreat he went over to the map and talked to the general from there. Lifting his hand, which still held the glass, he waved it over the expanse of wall.

"These lines that are so simple here, these little marks on paper, are bought with men's blood. How many strong young lives were lost to give us just this little! You and I, General Pissarjev, are old men. Our lives are not worth very much. But it is we who transmute heroism and sacrifice into the imperishable gold of Knowledge. We must not let one grain of it be lost!"

17. EPILOGUE

THE DELISLE MAP, made out of Louis's distaste for figures and Joseph's love for Louis, had a long popularity. Its scholarly confusions revived the hope for a northwest passage, and long after seamen knew the west coast of America, landsmen bought this map. Led by the poetry of Joseph Delisle, these men pushed across the interior of Canada and Alaska, mapping the country and finding furs and gold.

George Steller's work had even greater success. By the close of the century his book, *The Beasts of the Sea*, had been translated into the spoken languages. It could be found along the wharves at Amsterdam and Marseilles and Plymouth. The little man with his pride and his malice was gone. The keen eyes and the tireless devotion to science lived on in his writ-

ings. And men like Khitrov, captains who had never read
another book, pored over Steller's words, their eyes darkening
with wonder.

For fifty years the Russian trader ruled the islands alone.
During that time the sea cow, the sea otter, and the brown-
skinned Americans were destroyed. But by 1800 new men
were coming north, following the stories of George Steller.
The white sails moved around the Horn and up the coast of
America. They passed north of the trade winds, north of the
clear water, and into the fogs beyond.

A few decades and a new ship appeared among them. A
ship with strange, sleek lines, a miracle of design, a miracle
of swiftness, the wonder and the envy of the sea, the Yankee
clipper. Yankee poachers were slipping through the fog, steal-
ing the seal under the very guns of its lawful killers.

By 1860 the Russian revenue from this territory had dwindled to nothing. A report made to the czar that year stated
that the territory was worthless to Russia and that her efforts
to maintain her rights there were "alienating the good will
of a friendly people." The report advised selling it all to
the Americans. "Let them have the mainland, the Aleutians,
and the islands in Bering Sea. But let us retain the Commander
Islands so as not to have them too close to us."

The matter was broached secretly in Washington and secret
wheels began to turn. It was necessary to organize an American fur company with senators as stockholders. This had
been done by 1866. On March 31, 1867, a treaty for the purchase of Russian-America was sent to the Senate and was
ratified eight days later.

The press, which knew little about Russian-America and
nothing at all about the fur company, had a great deal to say.
The pro-administration New York *Times* flew to the defense
of the treaty. It discussed the vast resources of the territory,
chiefly timber and coal, and added that there was a "dwindling

fur trade which may be resuscitated by American enterprise."
Another advantage was the chain of islands, convenient steps
to the newly opened door of Japan. "We can send our citizens
from this shore to the Asiatic coast in open boats, never
being exposed to any peril whatever." But the chief merit of
the treaty seemed to lie in the fact that it would give offense
to Great Britain. "The English representatives here are deeply
chagrined and are expected to protest the treaty," said the
Times.

The anti-administration New York *Tribune* took the same
view of the matter. It claimed that the administration was trying to divert attention from its domestic difficulties by plung-
ing the country into foreign complications. "We have no
occasion to be dealing in impertinences!" it cried. "We have
put ourselves in the attitude of seeking ostentatiously the
friendship of a Power not friendly to England and of con-
tracting what is tantamount to an alliance for the sake of an
affront."

The British press was unaware that the purchase affected
Great Britain in any way and had no comments to make.

But the treaty had been ratified. Russian-America was re-
named Alaska and made a military district. The following
September, General Davis, with two companies of troops, left
San Francisco to take over the administration of the territory.
Mr. Hutchinson of the American Fur Company went with
him.

The ceremony of transfer took place in Sitka on October
eighteenth. The Russian flag was lowered and the Stars and
Stripes run up in its place. The Russian governor ignorantly
turned over his property to Mr. Hutchinson of the fur company instead of to General Davis, to the great annoyance of
General Davis. But he had turned it over. The control of the
islands had passed from the government at St. Petersburg to
the government at Washington.

CPSIA information can be obtained
at www.ICGtesting.com
Printed in the USA
LVHW050721110522
718474LV00004B/292

9 781013 685699